CHILD OF THE WINDS

My Mission With Raoul Wallenberg

by
AGNES ADACHI

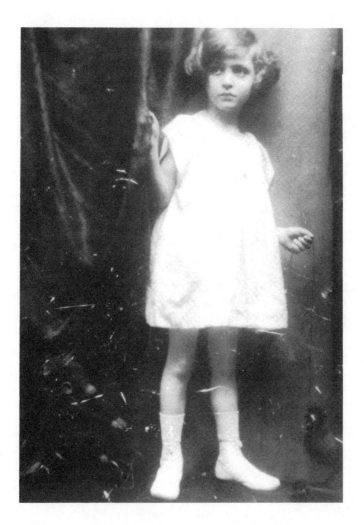

LIBRARY OF CONGRESS
CATALOG CARD NUMBER 88-83367
ISBN 0-9621930-0-3

ADAMS PRESS
CHICAGO

PRINTED IN THE UNITED STATES OF AMERICA

Dedicated to His Majesty
the late King Gustav V of Sweden
and
Raoul Wallenberg

ACKNOWLEDGMENT

I am indebted for writing this book greatly to my husband Masa, who listened and encouraged me through our 28 years of marriage always being behind me with suggestions and emotions I was not quite sure of.

In later years my two sons Taro and Jiro read and corrected my papers.

My thanks goes to my daughter-in-law Bonnie, who patiently edited the finished product.

For editing I am most thankful for my dear friends Marjorie Gill, Diane Berg and Ruth Swayze, who all felt comfortable reading it.

Deep thanks goes to my secretarial worker, Diane Mc Ginley and her husband.

Without all of you I could not have done it.

PROLOGUE

Absorbed in thought, totally drained of emotion, my arrival to the United States was suddenly disturbed by a voice.

"Agnes, do you smell it?"

I turned my head to see the smiling face of one of the officers of the cargo boat in which I was traveling.

"What smell?" I asked.

"Boston baked beans," came the laughing answer.

Yes, indeed, there was the smell of Boston baked beans, but there was also the smell of "freedom" which only I could smell. It has been a long, hard road, but in retrospect every minute lived was worthwhile for this arrival and the life that lay ahead.

Sitting on the rolling hills of Marlboro, Vermont, my life passing before my eyes, glorious music fills the air. I have to put it all on paper. My husband and sons encouraged me to write it all, the good and the evil, the failures and the achievements.

Life would probably have stopped for me and many thousands in 1944, if there had been no

Raoul Wallenberg, who gave his youth and freedom for our lives. Without him there is no story. Without him and his legacy we could not fight today and in the future for freedom. He made me human, strong and caring.

I am a child of the winds. I was blown all over the world, but now I have stopped. Now I live for my family, and for giving the world's young the teaching of my friend, Raoul.

Agnes Adachi

CHILD OF THE WINDS

CHAPTER 1

My Mission with Raoul Wallenberg

The late 1930's had me globe-trotting between my native Hungary to Germany, Italy, England, France, and in 1939 I lived in Switzerland. For many reasons Switzerland was the choice at that time. I had a big family in Zurich, and very dear friends in Geneva where I wanted to be to perfect my French. I lived with a family as a"mother's helper" which gave me free lodging and food, and, at the same time, enough time to study, date, listen to good music and ski.

I was busy at that time writing poems, and one of the best I wrote in Diablerets, an Alpine village where I went with this family for winter vacation.

One evening I opened my window and from my lighted room in the dark night, I saw the reflection on the Alps of a figure of a devil. I even saw the horns. It seemed so much alive. I had a kerchief on my head, and the ends stood up like horns. It was really frightening, so immediately I wrote a poem titled: "I saw the Devil himself."

The greatest cultural event in 1939 was the

moving of the famous Prado Art Museum from Madrid to Geneva...wall to wall were paintings, brought there while the Civil War ravaged the country from 1937-39, a war in which General Francesco Franco emerged as a dictator with the help of the Nazis and Fascists.

The Prado Art Museum had the world's richest and most comprehensive collection of Spanish paintings, but also Italian and Flemish art. Housing these incredible treasures took its toll. The responsibility was so great that the Swiss curator committed suicide. I was grateful to see the collection in Geneva, as it was displayed magnificently, lit in the right way so that one could see every detail. Much later I saw it back in Madrid, but it was dark and cold there.

Geneva was a great place in which to live. In the summer of 1939, with not a care in the world, I made a tour from Switzerland to France and back with other students, sleeping in youth hostels, meeting other foreign youngsters, having the experience of trying to learn each other's language, songs and dances. We had no enemies, just friends, and no politics on our minds. Christians, Jews, Moslems, Arabs, Buddhists---what a cluster of youth! Right then we could have run the world in peace.

It was a very picturesque trip. It was to St. Gallen, Aix les Bains, then Grenoble, nestled in the surrounding Alps, which fast became our favorite student town. Next came Valence, and another favorite, Avignon, then Nimes, Ville Neuf, Arles and Marseilles, the wonderful port city of France, Casis on the Riviera, Provence, then Rue des Alpes on the way back, Gap, Grenoble again, and Campery, Annecy and Geneva.

After this great trip our arrival back in Switzerland in early September was therefore more shocking than anything we had experienced before.

In Geneva a Zionist Congress was in progress, and lots of people took time out from the meetings to come to the beach of Lake Geneva for a well-deserved rest. The majority of these people were from Poland. As they sunned themselves in peace, seemingly without worries, suddenly, like lightening, the microphones blared the terrifying news that "Germany had overrun Poland." It was September 9, 1939.

We could hear a pin drop in the sand. The terror in the faces of the Poles spoke of death. Panic broke out. "Our families are back in Poland" we could hear them say. "What to do?" With half-naked bodies they ran to the phones, post offices, railway stations.

I felt my heart stop. I could do nothing for these people. No words could help. Right there I promised myself to work for peace with my utmost ability. I felt I must survive to

3

help! Little did I know that in a small way, in a few short years I would be able to do just that. That I would meet Raoul Wallenberg, that my family and I would survive, and that I would be able to help others. Never did I imagine that Raoul, for his great humanitarian work would suffer in the Russian Gulag for over 40 years.

I figured that from neutral Switzerland it would be easy to work for peace. My friends in Geneva thought otherwise, telling me to go home to Budapest. They felt that there was no way that Hungary would also be overrun by Germany. I respected their advice and went back on my father's birthday, January 21, 1940.

Plenty was going on. From Germany and Poland the Jews were taken to the gas chambers. We did not believe it! Few escaped in time to take refuge in Hungary - the lucky ones made it to America, England, Switzerland and Sweden. In no time Czechoslovakia was taken and people came to us. Our home became a haven for many.

In spite of all this happening, we still were optimistic that Germany could not go on, and that the "neutral" countries would not allow millions of people to die by the hands of these butchers.

1941 was an unforgettable year on the whole. Hungary still was not in the war-path directly; the trains were running, mail was still arriving from other parts of Europe.

We waited at our railway station for a train from Berlin, hopefully bringing my mother's best friend, a widow, Aunt Rosa and her two daughters Anita and Lydia, both friends of mine. As their father was Hungarian, they lived in Budapest, until his untimely death then moved to Berlin where Aunt Rosa had the means to bring up the family comfortably. Their brother, Gus, was already in England. With lots of correspondence we begged them to come back to Budapest to us. Finally, one afternoon, my father went to the train station by himself. I so clearly remember. It was Friday afternoon. Suddenly he called to tell us that the girls had arrived alone. Aunt Rosa was not with them. The girls assured Papa that she would follow soon. It took her over six weeks to arrive, but thank God she came!

Anita was 16 and Lydia 12. As they were very religious we had to have special foods for them. Both stood at the window crying, staring out to the lighted streets, where people still walked and shopped. In Berlin there was mother, and it was dark after five. The war was on! It was great to have them, for I gained two sisters. Anita was tall, blonde, blue-eyed, extremely talented in languages, acting, handy works and so on. On Sunday morning she was already doing millinery jobs for friends of ours and fixing runs on silk stockings. At that period of time this was fashionable work. Silk stockings did not have to be thrown away. They could be fixed. I also got her a job teaching children German and English. As she earned a little money, together we could belong to an English club run by South Africans. Needless to say all the young men were madly in love with her. Anita's story does not end here.

Lydia was dark-haired, brown-eyed, very graceful. She too could act and dancing was her dream. Lydia was enrolled, not very happily, in a school to learn weaving, which my mother wanted her to learn as a profession.

After Aunt Rosa arrived we went looking for an apartment. We found one quite far from us, but that gave me the chance to go out there every Friday evening to turn on the lights, as Aunt Rosa was very religious and in 1941 we had no automatic light switches. That apartment brought luck to them. I will tell you about it later.

Myself? I was giving English lessons to young children. One of them was a little girl named Agi, a lovely nine-year-old, the double of Shirley Temple. Today she is the wife of Congressman Thomas Lantos and a grandmother. Together they were responsible for starting to look for Mr. Wallenberg, and instrumental in having a resolution passed in Congress to grant honorary United States Citizenship to Raoul Wallenberg, the third individual so honored in the country, which President Reagan signed into law on October 5, 1981. It took close to forty years for us to meet again.

In Budapest, however, in the 40's, we walked around talking English, even though it was not proper to speak foreign languages, especially English. We walked in the streets as foreigners, as if we had just come from New York or London. It was dangerous, but fun. American and British films, however, were still popular.

My correspondence with foreign friends was considerable. Very often I received letters from a Swedish friend whom I had met when I was in high school and as a girl scout with knowledge of languages I had become a tour guide. A young man, by the name of Toto, took one of my tours. He told me he was an engineer from a small town called Orebro, in Sweden. In many letters, he told me how fond he was of me. Never in my wildest dreams would I have believed that I would be saved through Toto, and through him I would meet Raoul Wallenberg and be able to save other human lives.

At the beginning of 1943, I stopped giving English lessons and worked and learned the hotel business in our then famous Ritz Hotel - the famous rendezvous place of abdicated King Edward and Mrs. Simpson. With the ever growing foreign Jewish population we began to worry more, and we looked for signs of unrest. At the end of 1943 it was obvious that our days were numbered...but there was nowhere to go. We had Czechoslovakian and Rumanian Jews in our home, and through friends, we gave shelter to two French underground men, John and George, two fine men - John a French peasant, George the learned one. They were parachuted into Budapest before the March 19th, 1944 arrival of German troops, with the purpose of learning what the Germans were up to, and to kill as many as possible, and to act as couriers between the Allies and Hungary. We admired them for bravery, but they thought this very natural. After all, France wanted to keep her independence too. Sometimes we did not see them for weeks and we worried, but when they arrived back, there was both satisfaction and fatigue on their faces.

At that time I had an identity problem. My father believed that all human beings were created equal, regardless of religion, color or creed. I knew that I was a Jew, but knew nothing of Judaism. I was educated in a Protestant (Reformed Church) school, where the reformed church teacher, my favorite educator, took it upon herself to teach me what I had to know about my religion, and a little Hebrew. In the process, I learned everything there was to know about the Protestant religion. In my life the only religious part was the Friday night candle lighting, when mother, who believed more in religion than papa and I, did give us weekly blessings. Christmas was the big holiday in my life, with the glittering Christmas tree and giving presents to those who were less fortunate than we were. It was a celebration, not a religious event.

The principal of our school then was Albert Berecky, a grand and highly respected clergyman, who later became Hungary's Protestant bishop. He had six daughters. I was friendly with all of them. I spent much time in their company, so I became like a seventh daughter! Bishop Berecky was the first to try to save my life.

When times became tougher, I really did not know where I belonged. I felt I belonged to the world. Working in the Ritz Hotel was a great experience. I had to learn everything, starting out in the kitchen peeling potatoes. There is a special art to peeling them so that it looks uniform. We don't think that necessary, do we? But there it was. I had to learn this first. Then, came making new salad recipes, making gourmet dishes, and working with French chefs.

My great pleasure was in writing a poem in French, right in the middle of a new creation on a greasy piece of paper! I wrote this in French especially to an Italian businessman who was in Budapest just then. And I was very much in love with him. In my very limited spare time we had secret meetings, but unfortunately he was married. Hungary had strong "morals" and this was not anything anyone would have approved. He never had a chance to read that poem in Budapest, but after the war in Italy he did.

After my experience in the kitchen, I was promoted to the offices to learn the management

of as big a hotel as the Ritz. In a way I was a
great asset to the hotel as I spoke fluent
German, French, and Italian as well as
Hungarian. In the office, however, I was not
very popular, being an associate to a one-legged
man who was eating Jews. He could not do too
much harm at this moment, as I was a friend of
his girlfriend who was an old friend of mine.
She brought me to the Ritz, and I was a pet of
his boss, Mr. Marenchic, Everything went fairly
well until the day of March 19th, 1944. That
was the day life crumbled at our feet.

I remember the beautiful morning, sunny and
cold, when a very excited neighbor of ours ran
to us, telling of the BBC announcement that
Admiral Nicholas Horthy "Administrator of the
Realm" would soon be on the air to announce the
break with Germany and that we had joined the
Allied forces. My father ran for the champagne.
I begged him not to do it, as somehow I would
not believe in our great good fortune. He told
me I was too young to understand, so he poured
the champagne. The Admiral came on the air. In
a few simple words, he announced the intention
of the Hungarian Government to break with
Germany. He got about that far with his speech,
when suddenly he was interrupted by the Nazi
anthem and Horthy's voice disappeared. There
had been a takeover! I spilled my drink, turned
and ran to the Ritz.

When I got to the street it was still
beautiful, but the sky was darkened by

airplanes. I thought they were American or British.

When I arrived at the Ritz, I was immediately summoned to Mr. Marenchic's office. He spoke to me in French (he spoke sixteen languages) and told me that there was a take-over by the Germans, The airplanes I had seen were German. Horthy was captured. "Please go home to your parents. I don't want them to take you from here." Tearfully we kissed and he blessed me.

I ran with terror in my heart. I made it home and papa quietly said, "You were right."

The terror started immediately. Every hour of the day different announcements sounded on the radio. Of course, one of the first forbade listening to the BBC, but everybody did.

Surprisingly, we were not collected from our apartments or houses yet, but we knew it was only a matter of time, since 45,000 Jews had already been taken from the countryside to the gas chambers.

All I could do at this time was to read or listen to some short wave radio station, which I could find easily on my big radio. There was always something interesting to pick up that way, and so to learn what was going on in the outside world. I missed my job at the Ritz, and missed my friends, Anita and Lydia's company.

It was a terrifying feeling that one was so
helpless. One hardly lived, and life could end
so suddenly, as it already had for so many
thousands.

Unfortunately, Anita had no telephone, but
in the house where they lived was a leather shop
run by two brothers, Zoltan and Istvan, and as
they had a phone, our friends could always make
a call or receive one. Zoltan was already ready
to find an excuse to see Anita, and he soon
asked Aunt Rosa's permission to take Anita to
the theater or to the movies. There were still
no stars on our clothes, or curfews for Jews, so
there was a chance for a little good life for
Anita.

However, this happiness could not last.
The day came when a new announcement came over
the radio that married women could not be
deported. Ridiculous, but we wanted to believe
it. Zoltan went to Aunt Rosa at once and
offered to marry Anita, with the promise that
right after the war they annul the marriage. He
also told them that he was going to move with
his mother and brother to a neighborhood where
there were no Jews. They would also have false
papers and he wanted Rosa and Lydia to live with
them. He promised that he would take care of
everything.

This wonderful man loved Anita so much that
in his mind nothing was impossible. Anita was
desperate that she should have to get married at

such an early age, but Aunt Rosa was hoping to
save one of her daughters and agreed, though not
to the part about moving with them. They were
married by a Justice of the Peace and Anita
moved in with us for two days. After that they
went to their Grandmother's apartment. Zoltan
did move, but every week on Thursday he met me
in a little park, bringing from God knows where,
kosher butter, bread and fruit for me to deliver
to Anita, always with the message to please
come, that the neighborhood was ready to accept
his "estranged" wife. There was always a great
"thank you, but no thanks." Zoltan never gave
up his weekly bringing and asking. Finally,
later, they moved in with him. Needless to
say, after the war, instead of annulling, they
loved each other so much that they had a real
wedding. Today they are still happily married,
living in America, have two children and are
already grandparents! Aunt Rosa, Lydia and Guss
from England, are all here and we continue being
sisters and shall until we die.

After we settled Anita's fate, a new
announcement sounded and this time it was
against mixed marriages. Divorce, or the spouse
will be counted as a Jew. Within hours
thousands of couples committed suicide. What an
easy way to kill people! My youngest aunt and
her husband wanted to kill themselves, but
fortunately he called us and we talked them into
hiding instead of ending their precious lives.
They did just that and survived. After so many
people died, the Nazis called off the threat,

and announced that he or she will not count as a
Jew. Of course, for most of them, it was too
late!

A few week's rest again. One day our door
bell rang. Outside stood a young German
soldier. My heart stopped. Before I opened the
door I saw my parents' frightened faces. I
looked out again. The face of the soldier was
familiar. Suddenly I remembered. In 1936, at
the invitation of Aunt Rosa, I enjoyed the
Summer Olympics in Berlin. I met this young man
and exchanged addresses. He now found me, and
evidently my name did not tell him I was a Jew.
I had to open the door with surprise and an
unpleasant feeling at the same time. He invited
me to walk with him and show him Budapest. With
a sinking feeling I said good bye to my parents,
and without inviting him in, I left the house
with him.

I was hoping that I would survive this
without opening my big mouth to say something
wrong or give myself away. It was hard not to
have the urge to "kill" because, as we passed by
a synagogue, he suddenly mentioned how great it
would be to kill all the Jews. All I could
think of to say was in the way of a question.
"Why do you want to kill? Has any Jew harmed
you?" He looked at me and said calmly, "No, but
the world has to be rid of them so we can have
only Aryans and pure Germans." I ventured again
to say, "I did not think of you as a killer.
How can you do it?" His answer was, "I am a

14

German, and Hitler told me what to do."

Suddenly I could not stand any more. I
looked at my watch and said, in a panic, "Oh, I
am sorry I have to teach! Goodbye." I turned on
my heel and went. I have never seen him again,
and I hope maybe that the war and all the
suffering on his side too, was a lesson not to
kill people he did not know!

A short while went by until a new
announcement came over the radio, that those who
were of any other than the Jewish religion would
be safe. This was a surprise to all of us, it
was not something we could have believed, but
life was precious and again we wanted to
believe. Next day my dear Principal, Pastor
Berecky, came to our house and told my father
that he wanted to baptize me as a Protestant in
the hope that this would save me.

Naturally my papa said, "Yes," and together
we went to the church where, in a small chapel,
Pastor Berecky baptized me. It was not an
ordinary baptism. It was more tears than water.
It was as if he baptized a new seventh daughter
of his own. I could only be very humble in his
blessed arms. I am sure that his wise words and
blessing did help my survival. Pastor Berecky's
parish saved many Jewish lives, hiding them in
the church cellar. How I respected and loved
this man.

Yet a few years later, when he became a

15

Bishop of Hungary, he was sent as an emissary to the United States. I was here, safe and well, and in a few weeks I was to become an American citizen, but I was advised not to see him. After all, I was told, he represented today's Hungarian government. Foolishly, I listened. I was a coward. Raoul Wallenberg would not have been a coward. He would have thanked a friend like Bishop Berecky. I do hope that someone in his family will read this and will find forgiveness for me. I really loved him, and will never forget what he thought of me, and how he risked his life to save mine.

Now I was a Protestant. I wore the Star of David on my clothes, and we still lived in our apartment. To this apartment one morning the mail brought two letters which changed my life overnight. I still wrote poems and was really anxious to publish. I wrote under a pen name, which was "Rolopa." This was the abbreviation of Rome, London and Paris. I did finally send my work to one of our best papers, Ujsag (which means "news" in Hungarian) though with not much hope of getting an answer. It was a very prestigious paper. But that morning the letter was from Ujsa. Not only was it from the paper, but from their Editor, who was a very famous man himself called Mr. Makay. I have no idea how my poem got into his hands, but the letter said the following:

Dear Lady!
Your poem is wonderful and real---

but---unfortunately the censor
will not allow a poem with such
substance to be published.
I will put it with my memories.
Yours truly.

This, coming from him, was more than if my
poem had been published, and it was written by
hand!

The second letter was a small white
envelope, very unsuspiciously printed "Swedish
Legation" on the back. As I opened it my hands
were shaking. They asked me to come and visit
the Legation as soon as possible. I was
dumbfounded, confused. I could not imagine why
they wanted me, and also how I would get there.
It was quite dangerous to visit foreign
legations. You can imagine, however, the
excitement in my family.

We had a dear friend, Pista, who was not
Jewish and who already had shown us how much he
cared for our family in many little ways. He
had a big black Mercedes Benz. So he put the
Nazi flag on it and whisked me up to the
Legation.

I was ushered into Minister Danielson, and
Mr. Mezey, the Hungarian Secretary, introduced
me to him. Minister Danielson was very happy to
see me. He knew that it was not easy to get to
a foreign legation.

He then started to explain the most bizarre story I had ever heard. He told me first about the very brave King of Denmark, who so wonderfully defended his Jews by telling the Germans that they were Danes, not Jews, and he himself put a yellow armband on. Then he told me about Sweden's great King Gustav V, as the one who had sent numerous messages to our Admiral Horthy, asking him to save his Jews, to help them so that Hungary could hold her head up again, and saying that he and Sweden would help Hungary. The King went so far as to have proclamations made all over Sweden, asking that if anyone had relatives or friends or business connections in Hungary, would they come forward to the Swedish foreign department and they would try to help.

And now came my great surprise. My fiance Toto (I did not know I was engaged) went immediately and told them that if there had not been a war on, I would already be his wife. Therefore, as a Swede, would they please help me immediately!

I was absolutely speechless, with all kinds of thoughts raging through my head. All those letters from him all those years. The thought that he must have loved me. I could not believe this was happening to me. Then I heard Minister Danielson saying that now that they were responsible for me, I would stay at the Legation until they could find transport for me to Sweden.

I could not believe my ears. I had a bit of soul-searching to do. Was it right to leave my family? But I was young and I wanted to live so much! It was a hard decision to make, but the Minister's and Mr. Mezey's encouraging words suggesting that maybe there would be a way of helping my parents too, made me decide to stay. Poor Pista was as dumbfounded as I was, so he just drove away after wishing me good luck, and assuring me that he would look after my parents and the rest of my family.

It was a dream. They sent a secretary to my parents, and a letter of explanation from the Minister and from me, and later he came back with a change of clothes, tooth brush, etc. The Legation was on the Buda side, in a beautiful neighborhood on the of top Gellert Mountain, from where we could overlook the whole city of Budapest. I was given a lovely room with a view of the garden. Very shortly I found out that I was not the only guest of the Legation. Our most famous guest was the Nobel Prize winning scientist, Szent-Gyorgyi, under the name of Swenson. He was a great man, very much against Nazism, and they were looking for him. Eventually, with proper disguise, he was removed from the Legation to a safer place.

Also, there was a very lovely German Jewish lady with two little sons, who was married to a Swede. Later, with Per Anger's help, they got out on the last train to Sweden and much later

19

we became good friends in Stockholm.

In a couple of days I received an Emergency Swedish Passport, good for the whole world. I really thought I was just imagining all this. In my own country of birth, I turned into a Swedish citizen.

The days went slowly, reading, eating and sleeping, not really knowing what each morning would bring, for the Germans had the defense artillery right above us. Some American, British and Russian planes had already bombed the city.

During the three weeks I spent at the Legation my parents had to move out of our apartment, but fortunately not too far. It was my late grandmother's apartment, and also my aunt's and my cousins. The Hungarian Nazi Party, the Arrow Cross, decided that if every second house were to be a Jewish house with a big yellow star on it, the Americans would not bomb Budapest out of concern for the Jewish population.

They had miscalculated, so the Allied spy service must have been really good. The Allied forces hit all of the important Nazi strong points, naturally damaging much of the city in the process. Somehow we felt we had to pay for freedom, and we waited for those American and British bombers as liberators.

Little did we know that our "liberation" would be by an even greater and more lasting enemy - the Soviet Union.

Now, as the bombing increased, we had no lights, and we had the Nazis above us.

One lovely, crisp June day, Minister Danielson, the staff, and the "guests" decided to have a picnic on the front lawn overlooking the Danube and the beautiful city of Budapest. As we sat there peacefully, I looked up to the blue sky and saw beautiful black birds. Then somehow one black bird opened, and I saw an object falling. All I had time to scream was "Cover! Bombs!" We all ran for cover. The "birds" were American fighter planes, and as we had no electricity, we had no warning of this surprise attack.

Unfortunately German defense artillery above shot down one plane. The pilot parachuted, and he and his burning plane fell into the Danube. We saw it all from a plateau, but unfortunately the pilot could not be saved. The Arrow Cross picked him from the water and he was killed immediately.

After this surprise attack, the Jews were in for it. Pista came back and demanded my return as the Arrow Cross was counting heads every day, and my name was still listed with the family. All of them could have been killed. The Ambassador argued that I was under the

Swedish government's protection, being a Swedish citizen. I felt I had no choice but to return and try to protect my family. However I did not leave with Pista at the request of Minister Danielson and Per Anger, First Secretary of the Legation. I went down in a street car accompanied unobtrusively by a secretary who had to report back the exact location and house number of my lodging. Also I had to promise that since as we could go out once a day, I would call them daily. Thank God the telephone still worked on the street.

Reunion with my parents, aunts, and cousins was great, although I felt some resentment on all parts for the three weeks of heaven I had had and so I felt guilty. In everyone's minds was only one thing - the moment when the knock on the door would come, and we would be on the way to the gas chambers. Some people had already been taken from the house.

We also had very dear friends of my aunt living with us. The husband, Laci, was not a Jew, and so between Pista and Laci, we had some food on the table. In our desperation we listened very quietly to the forbidden BBC and I listened to Benjamino Gigli records.

Hardly two weeks later, when I dutifully reported to the Embassy that I was still alive, Mr. Mezey told me very excitedly to come as fast as possible as a new development had arisen.

My young heart jumped. I would persuade Pista to please take me to the Embassy again.

He did! The day was July 9, 1944, the day in which more change came into my life. For on that day, I met the greatest hero of my life - Raoul Wallenberg.

Picture by Thomas Veres.

(Permission by the Family)

Kappsta, Lidingö, Wisings grandparents summer home, Raouls birthplace.

Photo Thomas Veres.

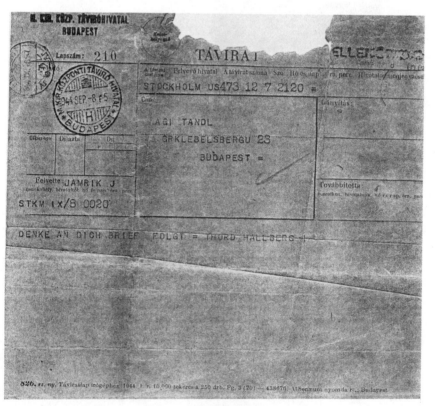

Telegram from my fianceé.

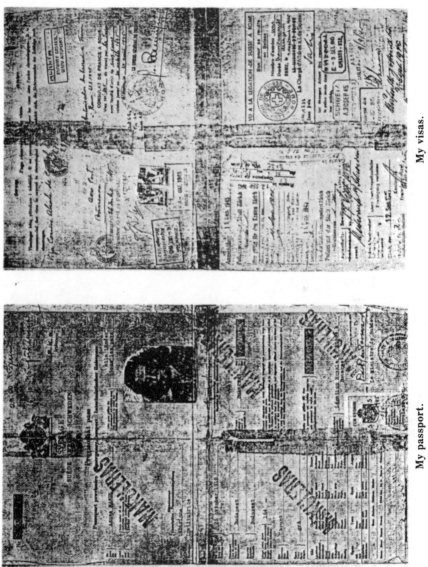

My visas.

My passport.

The "Schutz-Pass" Protective Pass.

My working paper with Raoul's signature.

CHAPTER II

As I walked into the reception room, there was Minister Danielson, Per Anger and a gentleman I had not seen before. It struck me that this person was unusual, with dark, piercing eyes. Mr. Danielson introduced me to Raoul Wallenberg. He was a Swede who was sent by the American War Refugee Board and the Swedish government, to organize a rescue mission for the approximately 280,000 Jews and anti-Nazi Hungarians still living in Budapest.

I looked at him with amazement. Somebody so young, so adventurous, yet, it seemed, so deeply disturbed. If I had known him better, and before, I would have known what a great and passionate man he was, a man who believed in justice, in love, in humanism. A man you could reckon with, a great organizer, a quick thinker and a brave man...at least he never showed us any sign of fear. He was a great leader, friend and brother to all of us who had the privilege to know him and to work with him.

He took over the leadership of the Legation so fast that we hardly noticed. This was not to everybody's satisfaction, but it was necessary. In no time he organized a working crew of about three hundred and fifty people from the Jewish community and some anti-Nazis. He divided the crews into "Section A" and "Section B".

As I stood before him for the first time,

24

not knowing who he was, he asked me if I would work with him and the Swedish Red Cross at once, as a receptionist. For the third time it seemed I was dreaming.

I said "yes," of course, but there were problems. I still wore a star, and I had the wrong lodgings.

A very confident smile came over the faces of the Minister, Raoul and Per Anger. Within an hour I had stamped by the Swedes and the German Nazi authorities a "working permit" with my picture on it, identifying me as a member of the "B" section of the Swedish Legation and member of the Swedish Red Cross, .

Furnished with this card, I had to go alone to the Police Headquarters to have my "star" officially removed. As I entered the great hall of the police station, my heart was beating so hard I thought everybody could hear it.

The police chief greeted me so warmly I thought for a moment that either I was dead or he was crazy. He took me in his arms and kissed me. Then he took a pair of scissors, and, while cutting off the star, said he was proud that he was the one who could do the honor. Yet how I despised the man, for I knew that he knew the Germans were about to lose and that the occupying forces would look into his past life, so the Swedes must have bribed him. He removed the star, and I turned and ran. Outside, I heard someone calling, "Another bloody Jew just escaped," but nobody stopped me and I got home safely.

Next on the agenda was our old apartment, which was in my father's name. I was told by Raoul and Per to go to the newly-formed housing commission and demand my apartment. I went, holding my head high, walking in and calmly telling the man I wanted the apartment back. He looked at me and gave me the paper without a word. I walked out slowly, wondering at the force that was governing my life. Why was I so lucky? Could it continue, or was it just the strong will of wanting to live? Or could the power of one man, Raoul Wallenberg, be so great that his touch was felt everywhere? Whatever it was, I was still free and about to get my father's apartment back!

Reaching my old home, I went to the superintendent who, for years, had lived on my father's generosity. He was not happy to see me but his wife was. I showed him the permit. At this point he said that his daughter was to have that apartment but his wife countered his reply saying that the daughter already had an apartment. I could feel the electricity in the room. Now all he could do was to send me to the house's lawyer and get his permission.

I went to the lawyer, who, knowing that it was only a question of time before the Germans lost the war, was more than willing to oblige,

for a price. I had promised to put his name
down as one who had helped and to act as a
witness to whom-ever the occupying force might
be, that he was not a Nazi. My contempt for
this human being was great but of course I
promised, though holding the reservation in my
heart that I would probably not do anything to
save him considering the atrocities in which he
was involved. But the permit was mine!

I walked back in a dream and went to the
superintendent, who, of course, could not
refuse. When we went upstairs, I had mixed
feelings. What would I find? How much would
have been stolen? What was left? To my great
surprise. only one room had been locked, and as
we opened it, everything - furniture, books,
paintings was there piled up. I stood
motionless, holding my breath, and again
thinking of my good fortune. This could not
happen. Then I slowly looked at the person
beside me who had lived as a leech on us for
many years, thinking that he did not have the
courage to steal.

I felt sorry for him, but only until
suddenly he gave me the keys and said, "I will
get even with you yet!" But at that moment the
ball was in my court!

In a day or so I got the telephone back and
of course this was a life saver; the Legation
could call me any time and I could call them.

27

Raoul started the organization immediately. His first idea was to have a Red Cross train go through Germany to Sweden, carrying the Jews of Budapest, but Raoul's conferences with the Hungarian government were fruitless, as the authorities would allow only 5,000 people to leave.

Then he brilliantly sat down to design a pass. Raoul was a first class architect and draftsman. The pass was designed in the Swedish colors, with the Swedish Crowns in the middle. On the right top was space for the holder's picture and signature. Above, it said "SCHUTZ-PASS", which means "Protective Pass". On the left, in German and Hungarian, was the holder's name, place and date of birth, height and color of hair. Under the Crowns, again in both languages, it said:

"The Royal Swedish Legation in Budapest confirms that the above-named in the picture, is authorized by the Royal Swedish Foreign Ministry to be repatriated to Sweden The concerned is registered also in a collective Pass."

It also stated in both languages:

"Until departure, the above-named and his apartment are under the protection of the Royal Swedish Legation in Budapest.

Validity: 14 days after arrival to
Sweden."

Furnished with this new document, Raoul
tried again to negotiate with the authorities.
This time it worked better for they allowed
about eight thousand, which in a short time
became twenty thousand and then thirty thousand.
As Budapest is not a very big city, the "grape-
vine" quickly spread the work like wildfire and
people were lining up at the Legation to meet
the Angel who was trying to help.

Within a week we had acquired from thirty
to fifty houses given to the Swedes by the
Jewish community on both sides of the Danube.
Raoul made them Swedish-protected houses by
hanging the Swedish flag outside so that they
became Swedish territory.   He put the
"protected" people into these houses and had
Nazi-clad Jews stand guard outside.   In his
book, With Raoul Wallenberg in Budapest, Per
Anger said, "The Swedish government was the
biggest landlord at this time in Budapest."

We also opened several offices in different
houses as very quickly not only Raoul, but all
of us, became targets for the Arrow Cross and
the Gestapo.

Raoul, just like King Gustav, enlarged
these passes and pasted them all over Budapest.
But even with all this help, the Arrow Cross
disregarded everything and took people out of

the protected houses through the basements.

Life was hard for Raoul especially, and also for his crew. I commuted between the apartment on the Pest side to the Legation on the other side in Buda on the Gellert Mountain to fulfill my duties as a receptionist or errand girl. I confronted lots of people who were strangers or whom I knew well. It was a great pleasure in either case to hand over the great "life-saving" papers. The exact number of people saved with these papers is not known. It is certain that more than 100,000 survived with or without the paper through the efforts of this unselfish human being, Raoul Wallenberg.

He was going night and day, in constant danger from all parties, and yet he never despaired. He never gave up! He even persuaded the Swiss Consul, Mr. Lutz, to give out Schutz-Passes. The Portuguese and the Spanish and the Papal Nuncio also issued identification papers similar to ours. Raoul gave his new crew a great reception on August 10th.

In a couple of weeks, Raoul opened his hospital and also a lovely orphanage in which he housed seventy-nine children. Hardly was there a day when he did not visit them. One day, after being away somewhere saving other people, he arrived back in Budapest to find that all the children but one had been brutally killed by the Arrow Cross men. This was the first time we saw Raoul really desperate. He went down on his

knees and cried. After a long while he got to
his feet and said that he would fight on,
because he wanted to "save a nation." I begin
to understand today what he meant by that. His
idea was to save all the children of this world
by teaching them that there is no difference
between religion, color, or creed, that there
are good and bad people, and that the young
should hold hands around the world and govern in
peace.

I try to convey this today in 1988 to young
people. It seems to me they understand very
much what he meant, and I can see it all over,
in children helping each other and helping the
old. I feel that even if five in each school
class listen to me and do what is in their
hearts, the world will be saved just as Raoul
wanted it to be.

The one little boy who escaped the massacre
was hiding under a chair, and somehow managed to
get out the back door and on to the street,
looking for his mother, even though he thought
she was dead. He found her by chance they
survived in one of our "safe houses" and today
are in America.

In about the middle of September my parents
got their Schutz-Passes and I got them back to
our apartment, instead of into a "safe house."
Also, my cousin came to live with us. The
family from Switzerland had gotten her and her
mother Salvadorian papers. Unfortunately my

Aunt Margarite could not yet be with us, and we worried a lot. One night, however, we got a great surprise.

Our friend, Pista, without our knowledge, took his Mercedes with two friends with Gestapo uniforms and revolvers. They entered Aunt Margarite's house, making a great noise so that everybody was frightened. There was, of course blackout so no one could see them. They walked up to the floor where my aunt was and banged on the door, telling her to get just one suitcase and march on, which she did. She thought the end was here, as she could not see in the dark, and she felt the revolver at her neck. So she walked down the staircase and was pushed into the waiting car. Then Pista put on the light and with a smile said, "Let's go!" It took guts, just like Raoul's, to do something so brave. I often think of Pista and wonder what became of him.

Now that I had our apartment back and my parents with me, I was free to go out when I wanted and was no longer afraid. As Raoul gave me of his strength, and his example of what a person can do, I walked around holding my head high, and wearing dark glasses, so that nobody would recognize me. Raoul was out of town more and more. He went with his driver, Vilmos Langefelder, and his wonderful young photographer, Tamas Veres, who hid his camera and who recorded almost everything you see today in books. He photographed Raoul many times and many Red Cross members as we needed trucks to bring people back from the railway stations just before they were to be shipped to the "gas chambers."

Raoul would jump on the top of the cattle cars heading to the gas chambers, and demanded that the doors were opened because "Our protected people are in them and you have no right to take them. They are protected by the Swedish Government, so release them at once!" Out of his pockets he would pull real Passes, insurance policies and drivers' licenses...all this he did so quickly, while screaming at the same time at the people. Thank God they caught on fast and moved quickly. Before the Germans knew what was happening, Raoul's car and the Red Cross trucks were full of people were heading for Budapest.

On the outskirts of Budapest there was a death camp in a mason factory. When Raoul was told that three thousand people were cramped in there, he arrived in the middle of the night with doctors, nurses, hot soup and bread. He again reprimanded the Nazis and the Arrow Cross members for their outrageous behavior in entering the territory of the Swedes and taking these people.

My dear mother's friend, who was in this death camp, remembers when Raoul entered the room where approximately three hundred old people were crammed, sitting on the cold floors

33

without water, toilets or food. Raoul would touch each of them as he tried to step over them and assured each of his return. He gave them food and asked for patience as he had to save the young first but would return and take them to safety, which he did.

When the bombing of the city became more frequent, we had to stop what we were doing many times and run for shelter, while taking the children and the elderly to relative safety.

The streetcars were still running. One day as I got in one to cross to Buda, the bombing started. We had nowhere to go, as there were really no shelters, and it was hard to run into houses where the basements were already overcrowded. So bravely the tram went on, hoping we would not be hit. In the midst of the welter of noises, I heard a bird singing. For a moment I thought I was already in heaven; then I looked up and saw a cage with a canary in it next to the conductor. At my questioning glance, the conductor explained, "I love her and if I have to die, we will do it together."

The tram went on. The bird kept singing. The bombing stopped. We had survived.

Opposite our apartment house in Budapest was the Ministry of Culture, which in 1944 became Gestapo headquarters. In the middle of the courtyard was an enormous clock that I had looked at from my side of the street for many

With Mother age 3.

With Father age 5.

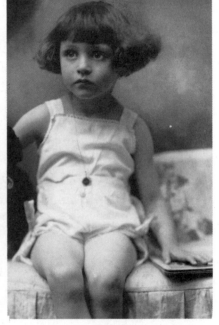

Age 5.

Egon and Me.
Konstantinople, Turkey, 1927.

Egon and Me.
Konstantinople,
Turkey, 1927.

With nurse,
Mother and us.

years. One afternoon, while coming home from
the Embassy after a heavy attack, I wanted to
see the time. In spite of my habit of many
years, something made me want to cross the
street. As I stepped off the curb, part of our
roof fell onto the street, just where I would
have been had I looked at the clock. Survival
again! What made me change my mind? This was a
miracle of life, of survival, still inexplicable
to me. Only some of us have to die; some of us
are allowed to survive, again and again.

After I recovered from the shock of this
near miss, my thoughts wandered back to my early
years, age seven to be exact. We were in
Turkey, in Istanbul (then Constantinople), where
my father tried to start a new life selling
radios after he lost his fortune in Hungary. At
that time you could listen to radios only in the
night, as the Turks thought them to be spy
machines. I was often left alone in the
apartment we had obtained through friends. As I
learned Turkish pretty quickly, I was the one to
do the shopping, always dressed in my little
silk dresses, hand-made in Austria. I was
unaware that children were still "sold" at that
time in Turkey, especially little girls. I am
sure my parents would not have let me go out
alone if they had known, As Fate wanted it,
next morning, while shopping for vegetables and
fruit, a young boy with his nurse approached me.
First in English, then in German, they asked me
who I was and where my parents were. I told
them my parents were at home, so they escorted

me back to the apartment. The nurse then told my parents what kind of danger their daughter could be in and she asked permission to look after me from that day on.

The young boy's name was Egon and, if my memory serves me correctly, he was the son of a Shell Oil executive from England. What a good time I had seeing the zoo, the parks and my very first movie, silent "Mickey Mouse."

By chance they also lived opposite us, so we ran a rope from their window to ours so that we could send messages if needed. One night as my parents were out selling the radios, I got a very bad toothache and put the light on. Nurse saw it and called over to find out what was wrong. After she was told, help came in a minute in an envelope, pasted to the string, containing two aspirins with instructions as to how to take them. In a little while I bandaged my head to keep the tooth warm. When my parents returned, they found me in bed, playing "Patience" with a deck of cards.

In those days I also learned the craze of the times, the "Charleston." One of our windows faced a floor of another building which housed a dancing school. I used to sit there, fascinated, watching them dancing the "Charleston." At that point, this was about the most exciting thing in my seven years of life since I was unaware of the dangers I had survived on the streets. So even as a seven-year-old, there was this strange survival. Maybe I had to be saved, so that in later years I should be able to work with Raoul and the Swedish Red Cross.

Day by day the air strikes became more destructive and that made the Gestapo angrier. Minute by minute more harm was being done to the Jews. They killed people on the street if they happened to be out. The radio made a new announcement that all young women between the ages of fifteen and twenty-five had to be in the sports palace the next morning by seven o'clock to work, cleaning up the rubble. But we knew better. This was a way to the trains and the gas chambers. Raoul asked all of us to come and write Passes for all the young women we knew, while he was again on the road pulling people from the death marches. We sat in a beautiful villa on the Buda side, near our still famous Chain bridge. By candlelight, we wrote the names belonging to the pictures and gave them to Minister Danielson to be signed.

Around midnight on this perfectly beautiful cold, snowy, moonlit night, With no sound outside because of the strict curfew, Raoul came in. He was tired, unshaven, maybe even hungry, but it was important for him to know that all of us were working hard to save more people. He told us everything must be delivered by three in the morning. Then, as an afterthought, he gave us a big smile and said "By the way, we have new neighbors, but you must not worry. It is only a

Gestapo headquarters." This was our friend and if he wasn't worried why should we be? I remember getting up shortly, with five hundred of these special Passes, bidding goodnight to all, and leaving for the Pest side. Clearly I can remember all I could hear was my lonely footsteps in the crisp snow, and the beating of my heart.

I delivered all five hundred, including one each to Anita and Lydia, and to a couple of other friends. All of this was very emotional, but highly rewarding. I was not even surprised that I had not been apprehended by anyone. My thinking was like Raoul's, that basically the Nazis and the Arrow Cross were cowards. They were the ones who were afraid to be out after the curfew. I thanked the Allies for not bombing on this lovely night so that we could finish our work.

When I arrived home I went to bed and into a deep sleep, only to be awakened suddenly in the morning by my darling Anita and Lydia. They had been to the sports palace and had shown their Passes to the German officer who said something nasty to them in German. They had turned and run, and the officer had let them go! Papa, who loved them so much, could not bear to see all his womenfolk crying so he put on his winter coat over his pajamas and left to buy bread. The girls, however, did not stay long. Anita decided to go to Zoltan and the same day she went with Aunt Rosa and Lydia to another part of the city where one would hardly find a Jew or suspect that one to be working for a hairdresser, as Lydia did.

A couple of minutes after the girls had left, our super came up asking where my father was. I told her that he had gone to buy some bread. She gave me a piece of paper which she said a man had handed to her. On it, in hasty writing, it said that Papa was at the Police station and needed help. It was around 8:00 a.m., so I called the Embassy. Raoul was there, ready to go off again to the death marchers. He immediately dispatched two embassy officials to assist me. We spent eight hours going to every possible meeting place that came to mind. In the meantime it started to snow and grow cold and windy. We did not stop until night when they delivered me to my home empty-handed, with the promise to begin again early in the morning.

I found my mother's door closed, so I knocked. She did not open it but called out, "Do you have your father?" When I told her we had not found him yet but would start again tomorrow, she sent me away. She would not see me. This was extremely devastating for me. It was a moment when I needed full support and love from my mother but all I could do was cry myself to sleep. Next morning very early, the officials picked me up and we left the house without a word. Half a day went by again. We looked in schools and other places that we had not yet visited. At last we went far beyond the

outskirts of Budapest to another sports palace.
I saw the diplomat go in and say "Heil Hitler"
and the German said something. The diplomat
came back in a rush and happily told me to call
home as my father should be there. We did, and
he was.

It seemed that when father got to the
street, a young Arrow Cross punk walked by and
demanded his papers. Father proudly showed him
the Pass, which this man did not accept. He took
my father into custody. In half an hour a
Gestapo agent walked into the police station
where he was being held.

My father ventured to speak to him in
German, telling him that he was under Swedish
protection. He was told to go home. This scene
was repeated three times, first by the Arrow
Cross and then by the Gestapo. Finally the
Arrow Cross won and they walked a long column of
people, young and old, in the snow and cold all
night to this sports palace. Again, in the
morning, after standing all night in the cold,
father went to a Gestapo man and he was finally
sent home. This time he made it, but not before
he had given his bread away to one less
fortunate. Another young man also went away
with his Swedish Pass. Father never went out
again, and Raoul was happy that the Pass helped
after all.

As the bombing increased, more and more we
had to go to the shelter in our house. There

were so many new faces! We did not ask
questions or names, just looked at each other.
My other aunt and her husband and daughter also
moved into our house since my uncle had a sister
living there and there was a place for them.
The American bombs went right through the house,
usually down into the basement. My aunts were
hit. It was a miracle they survived.

There was, however, one very interesting
face in our basement. There was a very good
looking gentleman, his wife, son and mother-in-
law. I could see that they were definitely
aristocrats. I wondered who they were, until
one day he asked me where I was going every day.
I had a good feeling about this man. He
introduced himself to me with his real name,
General Udvahelyi. I could not believe my ears!
Then he told me the story.

He did not want to fight with the Germans
nor did his son who was an officer in the
cavalry. In protest, he had tried to commit
suicide but he was saved. However the good
General left his home, took another name and
rented an empty apartment in our house, trying
to survive with the rest of us.

I found a marvelous ally whom I could
trust. It was a great pity he could not get
involved with us actively, but he did not want
to be on the street or be recognized. He had a
little short-wave radio so he could report to me
what he heard and I could tell him what I heard

at the Legation.   Eventually the young officer
and my young cousin fell in love. Unfortunately
this ended in tragedy, as my cousin died of
Polio after the war ended.   Right at this time
however, we tried to survive as best we could.

        The weather became colder and colder.   We
had one of the coldest, snowiest winters in
twenty years.   It was already December. Bombings
became more frequent.   Eichmann the Butcher
became obsessed with terminating all living Jews
in Budapest.   Raoul had to bribe, lie and scream
even more just so that he could save more lives.

        On the General's radio we were informed by
the Allies that the Russian troops were very
near to the Hungarian border.   (What they did
not tell us, was that we had been "sold" to the
Soviet liberators with the rest of the Balkan
states).

        The Germans knew that they were losing the
war.   Soon German soldiers began coming to us.
They told us that all their families had been
killed in Germany and asked for civilian clothes
so they could defect.   But just as we began to
feel sorry for these young soldiers, the
loudspeakers from the Nazi headquarters blared
lies over the streets of Budapest, assuring them
that the Third Reich was winning all the way.
The soldiers ran outside shouting "Heil Hitler"
and got themselves killed.

        One day in late December, just before

Christmas, as Raoul returned from his usual running around, he heard that the Arrow Cross was killing people in the Danube. They did so in the night, since it was very dark. The snow, however, was bright enough. They would bind three people together with a rope, so that they had to shoot only one in the middle and all would fall into the frozen Danube. Raoul was outraged. This was the first time that he needed our help too. He asked who of us could swim?

In a great hurry we collected our Red Cross trucks. Down we went with changes of clothing, hot drinks, nurses, and doctors. I never thought twice about what I was about to do. I stood fully dressed with coat, boots, and hat at the edge of the water, waiting for the sound of the gun so that we could synchronize our jumps with the bodies falling. I think that only three or four of us did this. We pulled on the rope as we could feel it stick to the ice got people out and into the waiting trucks and to Raoul's hospital. I think we only saved about fifty or sixty people but without Raoul they would have died.

This was the last time I saw Raoul Wallenberg. My troubles started. Every afternoon I began to have a little fever but I kept going for a while. Then the fever got so bad that I couldn't work. We didn't know what to do as it was not easy to find a doctor. Either they were fighting at the front, taking care of sick and wounded soldiers, or hidden somewhere.

Finally the super, my so-called "friend" who still wanted to get "even with me" for not letting him have my apartment, found a doctor. He came up and gave me sulfa with the biggest needle I ever saw. He said it was supposed to do me a lot of good, and left smiling. My reaction was fast. I threw up for hours. Mami tried a friend who found a hidden Jewish doctor, but by the time he came, I was in a coma. My mother told him the story of the last few weeks, including father's disappearance, running to the Legation and all the other problems we had experienced. This doctor told Mami that I had had a nervous breakdown, but didn't realize it. The fever developed when I was excited. Mother told him about the sulfa treatment and showed him the size of the needle. "Good God!" the doctor said. "This kid was poisoned! Simply poisoned. A needle like this is for horses, not people." Then we knew that it must have been a doctor who worked for the Arrow Cross, and this was a chance for the super to "get even" with me. In a few weeks he almost had another opportunity.

The doctor found an antidote. It worked, but left me jaundiced. There was nothing I could do. I was out of action! The doctor and my friends got me grapes. How and where they got them is still a mystery, but they helped a lot. The doctor was delighted to hear the story

44

of Wallenberg's work. He, like many people, was
in hiding. I made the doctor promise that he
would go to him, as I knew Raoul needed more
doctors that he could trust. He told me if
there was such a thing as a Red Cross train
still going, even if I had to go on a stretcher,
I would have to go. Of course that couldn't
happen.

While recuperating I had an interesting
visitor. One morning my parents announced that
a detective was there to see me. Someone had
reported, he said, that we were hiding Jews in
the apartment. He introduced himself as
Detective Deak. I got very angry and told him
to look under the beds and in the closets and
then, if he wanted to kill a sick person, to do
it, but quickly.

He then told me that he did not come to
look for Jews, but that he wanted to meet me.
He knew what I was doing, and all about
Wallenberg. He just wanted to say that he was
proud of me and asked that I tell the Soviets,
when they came, how good he was and how he had
never done anything wrong. I would think that
half the population suddenly wanted the same
thing! Very funny!

I had not seen Raoul since that night after
the Danube incident, but I got frequent phone
calls from the others at the Legation. They
filled me in on how Raoul had saved the ghetto
with 70,000 people in it.

Finally I was able to get out of bed. The bombing really got worse and worse. The Americans hit whole houses, the Russians only the top floors. Unfortunately, a Russian bomb hit our apartment just days after I finally could make it down to the shelter. Our shelter had the same disadvantages that other basements had. We had no idea if it was a heavy or light bomb when it hit. But we were all alive, so it had to have been a Russian plane. And so it was. Our apartment was hit. My room, with my whole library, crashed to the third floor.

That day we had to move down to our relative's place. We had quite a big family there already. My dear father risked his life to rescue my books from the rubble. He knew they were the most important part of my life. Today I still have them with bomb scars on them. Many years later, after my parents came to Sweden, the trunk with the books arrived first with them. I traveled with this treasure to Australia and then to the States. I arrived in this country with $500 in debts and a trunkful of books.

We heard on General Udvarhelyi's radio that Rumania was "liberated" and currently occupied by British, French and Russian troops. The General felt that we had to find a way for me to get there. I thought it was a great idea. The radio also announced that Rumanian citizens would be able to repatriate to their homeland.

He laughingly said that if I could become a Swedish citizen legally, that I surely could get illegal Rumanian papers. It was certainly something to think about.

We also heard that the Russian soldiers were stealing all they could and sexually molesting girls and women, even old ones. We really did not know what to expect.

On January 15th, it was unusually quiet all around. Suddenly the General called me down and very excitedly pulled me to the window. On the street, as far as you could see, German weapons were piled up on the ground. The Germans ran over to the Buda side. For quite a time we had lots of street fights, and bullets flew over to Buda and back to Pest. The Nazis did not give up easily.

In any case, the General and I hugged and kissed, hoping that all would be soon over. We were disappointed not to be liberated by the British or Americans, but we were hoping that this would not be too bad. Boy, were we wrong!

The Russians arrived and it was worse that we had expected. The officers rode in American Jeeps and wore American boots. The soldiers who had walked barefoot all the way from huts in Siberia washed their faces in the toilet and then relieved themselves in the bathtubs.

We girls had been hidden by our elders for

fear of attack by these wild soldiers. Most of them stole watches. Some had an armful of them and listened to them with great smiles while putting them to their ears to hear the ticking. We never thought of them as that primitive. They loved children. One of them stole my camera. He had no idea what it was of course and gave it to a little boy in our house who happened to know me well. He gave it back to me.

Many people were afraid for their little girls. A friend of ours brought her little daughter to us, asking if I could take her to some nuns who were taking care of children. I took that little hand, and we went out on the streets. I was scared out of my wits. The shells from Buda kept coming. On every corner there were street fights. We ducked several times, just missing the bullets. In the meantime I was telling the little girl a story to divert her from what was going on around us.

We made it to the nuns and I deposited her safely and made it back without being killed. The next day my friends decided that they could not be without their little girl and we smuggled her back out of the window at the convent.

The plumbing did not work too well any more. Since my father had to shave, I decided to go for water a couple of houses away where there was a big courtyard with a well. I was in the company of an old gentleman who came out of another house. We heard the whistle of a bullet

and the old gentleman fell to the ground.   I
heard his wife's scream from the window.

I cried and could not understand why him
and not me.   Spared again from certain death.
Only God knows why I was to live, but I was so
grateful!

The General and his son were picked up soon
by the KGB, which replaced the dreaded Gestapo.
We were so worried and did not think we would
see them again. In three days however, they
returned, telling us a fascinating but
frightening story of the ways the KGB held
hearings.   They were given lots of food and
vodka which the father and son tried to spill
rather than drink.   With a background of music,
dancing, and pretty women soldiers of officer
rank, they were casually interrogated.   They
were asked what they had done during the German
occupation and if our friend was really a
general in hiding.   They were tired, but happy
to be home again and unharmed.

This was when I decided life in Hungary was
going to be impossible, but I had to promise
father first to try and find a job in Budapest.
So after we had had all our shots for smallpox,
blackpox and typhoid I went to the newly made
employment office .

The first question was: "Are you a
communist?" Answer: "NO". Second question:
"Were you a Nazi or Arrow Cross?"   Answer:

49

"NO." Third question: "Well, what are you?" Answer: "Democrat, Humanist." No jobs for the likes of me!

Papa and Mama were not happy that I wanted to leave but I reminded them that I was to marry my fiance who had saved my life. How to get there or even to the Legation was a different story. Only boats were crossing the water as most of our beautiful bridges had been destroyed.

In a couple of days we got a surprise visitor - our dear Zoltan bringing us the good news that all of them had survived and that he and Anita would be having a real wedding soon. He came in a boat.

It was a great feeling to know that my best friends were alive, and I knew with Zoltan on their side, it could not be otherwise.

Now we tried hard to live on to see what tomorrow would bring. Food was scarce, but Pista and Laci still found some burned out food storage places to supply us with coffee and even sugar. I never liked black coffee, but never drank so much of it with so much sugar in it than at that time.

The days went by slowly. As we tried to rebuild our apartment, and organize our lives, suddenly the next miracle happened!

CHAPTER 3

We had more old people living in our houses than young and they preferred to sleep in the afternoon. We, the young mostly my cousin, Lydia, General Udvarhelyi's son and I went down to the basement for the duration. We talked and played cards. The problem was that the basement had only one exit.

One afternoon we were playing cards when a drunken Russian soldier came in asking for gold. We told our super to tell him we had no gold, not even gold teeth.

The super spoke Russian, and still wanted to get even with me. I don't know what he told the man, but it wasn't the answer he wanted. So, as it happened, just as I put my head down to pick up a card that had dropped, the soldier shot. The bullet went right over my head into the wall behind me. What makes people move at just the right time? Perhaps God was sitting on my shoulder.

I had ducked down so quickly and at so precise a moment, that the super and my company all thought I had been shot. They all ran out shouting, "Agi has been shot". My parents who were napping, came running down. It was quite a scene as they saw me come out dazed but unhurt.

A Russian officer had been called. He apologized, taking his drunken peasant away. I decided once again that I had to get out of Hungary. But getting out was not as easy as one might think. I still could not see even a way to get to Rumania. And if I did, what then? Where from there?

But again, as fate would have it, I got another visitor from the Buda side. He too, like Zoltan, came over in a boat. This was one of our friends, a Czech lawyer, who worked very closely with Raoul. He told me that members of the Legation were taken by the Soviets to Debrecen, the Soviet headquarters in Hungary. Dr. Paul Hegedus told me, as I already knew from General Udvarhelyi, that there was still a Swedish Embassy in operation in Bucharest, and perhaps the Minister, Reutersward, could help to relocate our Legation personnel. He said it would be wonderful if I could go to Bucharest and report to him. After all, he knew it meant a lot for me to help the Swedes. He did not tell me, however, that Raoul was not with the rest of the people, or maybe Paul did not know it. Of course I said "Yes!" immediately. My parents vehemently opposed it thinking quite rightly, that it was a rather dangerous mission.

I explained to them that it was my duty to His Majesty, the Swedish Government, the Legation itself and my fiance Toto. Of course this did not make them happier but it had to be done. Paul promised to get me Rumanian papers and he handed me a piece of gold telling me that I might have to use it for whatever reason. He was right. I did have to use it for many different reasons!

In a couple of days Paul did bring me the Rumanian papers, saying that I was repatriating to my "homeland". He wished me good luck and gave me the list of personnel who belonged to the Legation. He also gave me an additional list of seven Swedes whose location he knew and who wanted to get out of Hungary.

I was very excited. Now we had to find out when the trains for Rumania were leaving and I had to be ready for that moment. All I could take was a knapsack with my clothing and personal things. I hid my Swedish papers in my undergarments. I had only the Rumanian papers, my heavy ski boots which I had to wear for a month, and a fur coat. And, of course, I wore ski pants. It was very cold in February.

The whole city of Budapest fell into Soviet hands by February 17th. There was great chaos, little food, lots of illnesses, much snow, and cold. From one moment to another you didn't know what might happen.

Now the Russians, just as the Gestapo had, picked up innocent people on the streets and put them on trains to the Soviet. Some people just disappeared without a trace. Everybody lived in fear. The liberation of Hungary was a great disappointment.   I think if the liberation had been by the Americans or the British, I might have lived in Budapest for good.

My dear friend the General and his family were very sorry that I was leaving.   But they were also happy, feeling that there was not much hope for young people in Hungary unless they turned communist.

Finally the day came for good-bys from Aunt Rosa, Anita, Lydia, Zoltan and my family.   I went with Mami and Dad to the railway station. It was enormously crowded. We sat on the ground for nearly five hours.   Finally we got the signal for the train to leave.   You can imagine that those last moments were not the easiest. Would I see my parents again?   How would we correspond?   Would I be able to accomplish my mission?   Would it be dangerous?   Might it be easy?   It was all in the future.

I had to leave my parents smiling, so they did not know how broken-hearted I actually was. The uncertainty was so great.   There was no guarantee that I would arrive safely in Rumania. The train might be diverted to Russia.   This, thank God, my parents did not know. So my heart was full, but I was smiling.

I got a window seat and had a very nice couple as my partners. We sat there another hour before the train slowly began to move.   We were really on our way.   You could look around at the faces. I am sure many were not Rumanians, just like me. But no questions were asked. The destination was the same... or so we hoped.

After a few hours, some of us got hungry, and suddenly everybody came out with some food and very happily we shared all we had.

We went pretty steadily for almost eight hours. Then the train stopped at Szolnok and we were told to get out. Total confusion. We were told that we had to stay overnight. The train would go no further. We had to go on in the morning. We were put in an empty schoolhouse to spend the night. I put my fur on the floor. It was cold, but with all the people in there it soon became warm and when you are young, you can endure so much. I went to sleep immediately, and almost missed the call in the morning telling us that there was a train waiting.

Thank God we did move again. This time very nice Rumanian soldiers came into the wagons in which we traveled. No passenger cars were available. The wagons were filled with hay and we just sat on top of it. The soldiers told us that we would make several stops. When we came to the border Russian soldiers would check the wagons, and if they felt like it, we might be taken out, or transferred to a train back to Budapest or to the Soviet Union. So we were told to lie flat in the corners, not to talk or cough. It was not a great moment to look forward to but it was a risk all of us had to take. I am sure that many of these people were not Rumanians, but this was the only path to freedom as Rumania was already occupied by the French and British in addition to the Russians.

Well, here we were, tired and maybe a little bit frightened. Night came very fast and we arrived at the border. The Rumanian soldiers put their hands on their mouth and got off the train. We could hear the Russian soldiers coming. They were singing at the tops of their voices, drunk as they could be. The heavy doors opened and a flashlight just skimmed over the seemingly empty haystack. The doors closed again but still we did not move until the train slowly began to move again. We were in Rumania and hopefully the next stop would be the little border town of Aradin.

So it was that the train stopped and we arrived in Aradin. The station was rather dark, and somehow the people disappeared very fast. I stood there a few minutes more very still thinking of my two friends in Aradin. One, the Baroness Marika Von Neuman, who was my dearest friend, and had a home in Budapest but she had chosen to return to this small village in the hopes that it would not fall into the war zone. She was unmarried with a great family in Rumania. The two of us had met in the Budapest Gas Company, which at the time was one of the best cooking schools. She became the greatest philanthropist. I became the good cook.

Marika was a warm and great friend and a fine musician. You could not argue with her about a great composer or which Mozart piece was being played. She was involved in art, music and philosophy. In other words, she was the greatest friend one could wish for. Now that I had arrived, my first thoughts went to her, wishing and praying she was alive and here.

My other friend was a talented violinist who studied at the Liszt Academy in Budapest and lived in our house during that time. She too returned home in hopes of not getting into the war. Her address I knew well. I was just about to turn away from the station and try to find her house when a man came up to me and asked if I had just come off the train.

"Yes," I said.

"Do you have a place to sleep?" he asked.

I told him that I thought I had, and asked "But do you? And who are you?"

"A concert pianist," he replied.

That was a promising answer. I remembered that my girlfriends both had pianos. Maybe they could do something for both of us. So I told this man to walk with me to my friend's house and we would see what they could do. It was around ten in the evening. The streets were empty, but clean. The houses had windows and were quite well lit.

Shortly we arrived at the house. There was a big cobblestone courtyard and in the middle was a big piano. I knocked on the door. My friend opened it and even though I looked undernourished and tired, she recognized me at once. We screamed and cried with happiness. I told her at once that I had all my shots, inoculations, etc., in Budapest so that she didn't have to be afraid. But she really was not.

I introduced the stranger. She was kind enough to invite him in too. There was ham, bread and cheese. I could not stop eating, even though my friend warned me that I was going to be sick. How right she was! But it did not matter. It was so good. We told her about our adventurous trip from Budapest. She told us we were lucky. Many people went to Siberia instead and just disappeared. Yes, lucky we were.

Late into the night we talked. We did not sleep too much. In the morning we put our young man to work, practicing the piano. Of course the piano was badly in need of tuning, but even so it sounded quite good. A little later we had to go to a public bath where the nurses took care of those who needed to be de-liced and given inoculations. We did not need either, but the hot bath was a blessing. I brought along my one pair of silk stockings and high heeled shoes and when I put them on I could not walk, as for a month I had worn heavy ski boots. I really had to learn to walk again. We had lots of laughs out of this. On the way home I admired all the sweet shops and I am not a lover of any kind of sweets. But my body must have had a great craving for them. I had to stop at each of the stores and try something.

In the afternoon, nice and clean, I went to Marika's house. My heart was pounding in hopes that she would be there and would recognize me. I stood a few minutes before this lovely little baroque house before I had the courage to ring the bell. My Marika herself opened the door. Our embrace was as warm as it was with my other friend.

Marika had not changed. We sat and talked over the terrible war and what was still going on.   It was March 1st, 1945.   Both of us had lived through hell, but we made it. Our reunion was as though we had never parted.   I told Marika that I had to go to Bucharest. She told me that only people with official business could travel and asked me what mine was. I told her that for once I could not tell even her, but that it was very important and involved many people. Typical of Marika, she knew she could trust me. She said she would get me the official papers I needed.

Then we talked of how we could make some money. I told her about the concert pianist whom I had met and put at the untuned piano to practice. She said it was a great idea to have a concert as the people of Aradin were hungry for good music, and if he was good, it could certainly be arranged. I got up immediately and with her permission, I went to fetch Thomas, the pianist.

He sat down at Marika's marvelous piano and played Chopin. She was impressed. We had two concerts within two days and they were a great success. We split the money between us, so we had money for some clothing and food. Thomas practiced on Marika's piano. By the end of the week my dear friend Marika had the official papers for my mission to Bucharest. I had to leave at once. Thomas wanted me to stay and be his "manager" but something about him bothered me. Of course it was just in my mind, but suddenly I did not want to have anything more to do with him. He was devastated. I stayed firm.

After saying goodbye to my dear friends, Marika came to the station with me. I boarded the Express train full of Russian officers en route to Bucharest. Marika promised to come every Friday to Bucharest so we could spend some cocktail hours together. This already made me very happy as I knew no one in the capital city and was very uneasy what I would find there, how my mission would turn out, or how I would live. In any case, Marika was around me and that made me feel easier.

The train started to move. I looked around slowly in the compartment where I was sitting and found two Russian officers with me. This made me feel very nervous at once. But I thought of Raoul, and how he would have been courageous. After all, I was making this trip to help people. So the fear disappeared immediately. For a little while I sat there staring out the window, until one of the officers spoke to me in Russian. As I just smiled instead of answering him, he addressed me in German. I was afraid to answer, but I did. I said that I spoke German. He wanted to know where I was going. As the train stopped in Sinai, I said I was going to Bucharest. He wanted to know if I was Rumanian, and how I got the privilege of being on this train.

Inside, my stomach turned again, for I was not sure if this was a friendly conversation or an interrogation. I had to think very carefully how to answer.

So I said that I was Rumanian, and that I was going to teach in a school. At this point he introduced himself as Ivan, a medical doctor from Odessa. His friend, who could not speak German, was from Minsk. He was a writer and his name was Sergei. Ivan also spoke fluent English and French. Lunch time came close and the two of them asked no more questions, but shared their lunch with me. Of course there was vodka, but I would not touch it. After a few glasses of the vodka, they were drunk. I was again very frightened inside, but thank God the station of Sinai came and I excused myself and got off for a second of fresh air.

On my return the compartment was empty of the two officers. All they left was an overcoat and Russian book. The train moved again, and after about ten minutes the two arrived again. They looked harassed and sat down very quickly and locked the door. There was no conversation. The two just looked at each other for a couple of minutes and then suddenly they relaxed.

After quite a while Ivan started to talk to me again and to my great surprise he handed me a piece of paper with an address on it. He told me that if I needed them for anything I could reach them there, but only if it was an emergency. He also told me that their destination was Israel. Even though Sergei was a Christian, Ivan had some family there and they were trying to reach Israel.

As Ivan was speaking with me, I could see how tense Sergei was. He wanted to see my reaction. Slowly I began to understand that these two were dissidents and during the stop perhaps they were in hiding. The two could not have known that perhaps I understood the situation better than anyone. So at last I told them that I was a Jew, and that I was going to visit the Joint Distribution Committee which was helping Jews. It seemed they knew about that. After we reached Bucharest, we went there

together. Evidently Ivan had connections
already. I got a small job that at least gave
me some money to eat. The Committee also gave me
a room to sleep in. I said goodbye to my new
found friends, wished them good luck, and as
they knew my address, I told them that I would
be there if they needed help.

After a good night's sleep, I took a taxi
and went to the Swedish Embassy. The taxi
driver was very kind. He spoke some Hungarian.
He was not too happy to drive to the Embassy.
He said it was right beside the Russian
headquarters. Also he very kindly told me that
any time they might stop me and ask for
identification. He said he would come by later
to pick me up, and if he did not see me, he
would try again. That was really nice of him.
I explained that it was not necessary, but he
insisted.

It was a very beautiful, wide street, with
lovely trees and villas on both sides, this was
Embassy Road. Finally we arrived at the Swedish
Embassy.

I went in and a very nice Swedish girl
addressed me in Swedish. I answered in English,
telling her that I would like to see Ambassador
Rautersward. She asked me what my business was.
I told her that I could only explain it to the
Ambassador. She said that he was very busy and
asked if I could come back tomorrow. She said
she would make an appointment for me. But I

63

told her I had to speak to him today and I sat down on a comfortable chair.

She let me sit. She could see I was determined to stay, no matter what she suggested. Finally at four o'clock, she said the Ambassador would see me for a few minutes.

When the door opened, there was a tall, skinny, very frightened-looking gentleman. He asked me in English who I was. I immediately told him why I was there and who I was. He got so excited and asked so many questions at the same time that we both started to laugh and I tried one by one to answer them.

First I told him how I got to Rumania and how long it took me. His first advice was to be careful with whom I talked on the street or anywhere else. Then he took out a long paper that had just come off a teletype machine from Sweden. He found out that Toto, my fiance, was looking for me and then asked for the list of Swedes. I took out the list Paul Hegedus had given me. We found that we could tell Sweden that they were alive and of course, now he had to do his best to bring the Swedish Legation out of Hungary.

He was good enough to look through all my papers and very kindly advised me to throw away my Rumanian papers. He told me to register at the police station as a Swede. I told him that I had a room and a little job. He asked the address and told me to keep in touch by telephone. He also gave me some money, which he said I would return to the Swedish Government. I left shortly, much happier, hoping for my friends to arrive in Bucharest shortly.

Outside, as he had promised, the taxi man was there, but this time he had his little daughter with him. He told me that he was a widower and invited me to this house for dinner. I did not want to accept, but he was firm. So was the little girl. Reluctantly I had to accept and had a fairly nice time. He told me that he liked me immediately and his little daughter needed a mother. Well, I can tell you, for weeks he was after me. He brought me butter, bread, and cheeses. It was very hard to convince the poor chap that I didn't want to get married and settle down with him and his little girl, although I grew very fond of her. But I explained that I was engaged to someone else.

I telephoned Marika, telling her of my arrival and the job and room I had. She promised to come to Bucharest the first Friday she was free. Very shortly I also found that I could be a free lance writer for the Rumanian newspaper. I wrote quite a few articles. Food was expensive and the money I earned was hardly enough to feed me. So, most of the time I ate frogs legs that I could fish out from the river myself. I had some friends who already knew how to kill them and cook or fry them. It really is good food! I can't see why today in a

65

restaurant we have to pay a fortune to eat this delicacy when it can be taken from any river.

In a couple of days I found better lodging at the home of a very nice lady. There was a little balcony and the house was in quite a good section of the city and not too expensive. It was near the then famous Athene Palace Hotel. In this hotel was a good hair dresser who fixed my long hair when I finally had enough money.

The Athene Palace Hotel was also the place where they had a "caviar bar" like we have ice cream parlors in America. There were about five or six big freezers, each full of the finest caviar, even "Beluga," as the Russians occupied the city. My Marika came every Friday afternoon and we went to the "caviar bar" and chose our caviar. Then we went down to a cellar with wonderful butcher block tables. There we were served the chosen caviar on buttered toast with glasses of champagne. What a treat this was! Every week I could look forward to this very special afternoon with Marika.

One Friday afternoon I arrived too early for my usual meeting with her. I remembered I needed something from the tobacco shop where they sold writing materials and other things. While I was looking for my purchase, I heard a very familiar voice speaking to the cashier in French. I turned around and so did Jean Castanet my friend from the French Underground who had lived in our home off and on with his friend

George Le Loup. We were so happy to see each other again. Now that I knew there were French troops with the occupying forces of Rumania, it was easier to see why they came to Budapest. Our meeting was very exciting. He said that George was on his way home and hopefully, he too could leave for his home soon. Marika came then, and I introduced her to my friend. We had a great afternoon, the three of us down in the cellar, sipping our champagne and eating caviar.

I think it must have been eight or ten days after my arrival in Bucharest that my landlady got a call from Ambassador Reutersward for me to come at once to the Embassy. I went fast and there was Minister Danielson and the whole personnel of the Budapest Legation, except for Raoul.

After all the happy hello's and emotional hugs, I asked Per Anger where Raoul was. He told me that I should not worry. He would turn up. He told me the story of how Raoul wanted to do more for the people we had saved and took it upon himself to go to the Russian headquarters to see General Malinkov. Everyone had tried to talk him out of it but he was sure that he would get the help he wanted. He did go and in a week he was back in the company of two Russian officers on motorcycles. He spoke with some of his friends and to the Red Cross people, telling them that he had to go back to the General, but he didn't know if he was going as a guest or a prisoner.

67

However, Per said that as they had just heard that his mother had been notified that Raoul was in Soviet protective custody, he was sure that they would either bring him to Bucharest or we would meet him on the way to Sweden. Per said, "He also has his driver, Vilmos Langfelder, with him, so please don't worry. He will turn up as usual, in good health and full of jokes."

Sadly, today we know that the Soviets never let him go and that he is still in the Russian gulag 44 years later. But at that time we were optimistic.

At least now part of the Legation, minus Raoul, and the seven Swedes were in Bucharest waiting for further transportation to Sweden. Minister Danielson told me that I would get a little money each week to get me through the waiting period and they would take me with them to Sweden.

I was extremely happy to know that I would have the opportunity to get to Toto. Also they told me that he would have to pay back all expenses the Embassy extended to me. I was working as much as I could while waiting for our departure. I also met Ivan and Sergei again. They promised to help my parents when they went back to Budapest and they did just that a few months later, bringing them food, and offering assistance if it was required. They later helped my parents and Aunt Rosa and Lydia to get to Prague. Sergei had finished a book by then and he wanted me to take it to Sweden with me to have it published. It was an exciting prospect as it dealt with the current Soviet situation.

I made lots of friends in a short time and had a fairly normal life. One day, walking toward the Athene Palace, a Rumanian soldier stopped me and asked for identification. I quickly remembered Minister Reutersward's words, that I should not carry Rumanian papers, so I just smiled. Then he tried Hungarian. Still no answer from me, so he gesticulated so that I should understand that he wanted identification. I smiled again and handed him my Swedish passport which he could not understand, so he took me to the police station.

I continued my charade which frustrated this silly policeman a lot, but somehow they understood the name and phone number I put on a piece of paper and to my great relief they called that number.

After the policeman put the receiver down, I was motioned to a seat. I could not understand what was said, but sat there quietly. In a very short while there was some commotion and in walked a very worried Ambassador Reutersward. As soon as he walked in, before he could open his mouth, I wildly started to throw all the words I knew in Swedish, like "bröd, tack so mycket, mjölk, bröd..." which of course

means bread, milk, thank you." I repeated the
words over and over, gesticulating at the same
time. I could see the Ambassador's face begin
to relax. I was not quite sure if he wanted to
laugh or cry but he answered me in Swedish and
my reaction was of course to answer the same few
words. Then the police said something, and the
Ambassador held out his hand and walked me
outside to the waiting car. He burst out
laughing, and asked me how I got the idea to do
what I had done. All I could say was that it
worked. He took me back to the Embassy and
immediately gave me a new Passport and other
identification papers.

So the days passed with work, meeting my
friend Marika on Fridays at the Caviar Bar and
waiting for our departure. We were also waiting
for Raoul to appear. But he did not come.
Nevertheless, we were still confident that the
Russians would bring him to us before we left
the country.

Departure day finally came. I got the call
that we were leaving. The excitement was
wonderful. We all met at the famous Ploesti
Railway station. I say famous because it is in
the oil fields where there was heavy bombing by
all parties and much damage, but the trains were
running.

We, the eight Swedes and the Legation
staff, all assembled. The Russians started to
put the Legation onto the trains. We waited for

70

maybe a half hour. Then Ambassador Reutersward came and told us that the Russians had changed their minds and that the eight of us could not leave. Disappointment is not the right word. It is impossible to describe how we felt saying goodbye to the Legation personnel. Would we ever see them again?

One more moment and the train started to move and I heard Minister Danielson's and Per Anger's voice shout to us to be careful and patient. They also assured us that we would be meeting soon in Sweden.

Very heart broken, we left the station in utter disbelief that we still had to wait. That was March 1945. The trip took the Legation personnel to Odessa, Moscow, and finally to Leningrad where they went by ship to Helsinki and then Abo.

We returned to our lodgings, and thank God my landlady still had the room for me. Ambassador Reutersward still supplied me with money and again I tried some free-lance writing.

Then came May and the end of the war. It is strange that I have no recollection whatsoever where we heard that the war in Europe was over, or what my reaction was. I do not remember if we did celebrate or not. It is funnily enough like a blank spot in my mind.

However, the war was over and we were still

in Bucharest.   Life went on.   I had my visits
with Marika.   My French friend went back to
France to his family.

CHAPTER 4
FROM BUCHAREST TO ZURICH
MAY - SEPTEMBER 1945

For days and into weeks, we were expecting to leave Bucharest. Then, suddenly, we got our "marching orders" to leave in three days on a British military plane.

I tried to ready myself, filling my little suitcase, rather than the knapsack I arrived with. It was very exciting to know in my heart that I could leave this part of the world.

But it was also difficult to say goodbye to the many new friends I had made during my six months in Rumania. My landlady cried as did some of my friends. It was also worrisome knowing that even though you were leaving, anything could happen along the way and you might never make it.

The war was over less that a month and mass confusion still reigned.

I spoke to my two Russian dissident friends who wanted me to take the book one of them had written with me to the free world. It was a wonderful book, expressing so well what was really happening in the Soviet Union. They wanted the world to know that Communism did not work; that people were very hungry, jobless, frightened, and that the top Communists, the elite, had everything. They also wanted the world to know that the Soviet Union was not an ally of the Americans or the British. If Czarism was not good, Communism was equally bad. They felt that the time to expose the problem was now, that the world should end Communism!

I wanted very badly to bring the book with me. However we were warned that we would be subjected to an intensive search by the Russians at the airport and so I declined to take the book. I went to bed that last evening with a very heavy heart, feeling cowardly. I dared not take the book.

I was dreaming about my dilemma when I awoke suddenly to find two green eyes watching me in the dark and a furry body touching me. I jumped and so did the black cat, right out onto the terrace and to the street. Still shaken I decided this was a bad omen. Maybe once more we were not going to leave. At that moment I definitely decided not to take the book.

I should not have been superstitious of the black cat and certainly should not have been so cowardly as to leave this precious book behind. As it turned out there was no search. We were treated with remarkable politeness at the airport. But then, how was I to know this beforehand?

In the melee of tearful good-bys I almost missed hearing the honking of the big black

Swedish Embassy car taking one of our companions, Peter, the son of a most famous anti-Nazi Hungarian minister, to the airport.

It was a beautiful morning, the day we left. The sky was blue and cloudless. My young heart was jumping for joy. As we neared the airport we could see the twin-engined plane which was actually South African, not British.

Our baggage was weighed and so were we. It was terribly warm, but that took nothing from the great excitement of the moment.

At the last moment a young woman arrived. I don't know how she knew I was leaving. She was not a friend - just an acquaintance. However, she brought me a beautiful book of Rumanian art and I was very touched.

Then came good-bys from Ambassador Reutersward, and finally, and unbelievably, we entered the very hot, muggy, military plane.

There were eight Swedes, two French officers, and two Englishmen, one very skinny and one very fat. The fat one never took his eyes off me and never once put his brief case down. Why he looked at me without much sympathy, we only discovered later. For the moment, the voice of the engines was like music in my ears and I ignored his cold stare.

It was a time of pure joy mingled with

sorrow. I could not believe we were really getting out. Then my thoughts would go back to my parents in Budapest and what might happen to them, to my family in all parts of the world, and to my friends I was now leaving behind. Even now, in 1988, I don't know what happened to my two Russian friends. The last I heard, in 1945, they were in Budapest helping my parents and their friends to get to Prague, hopefully to transit from there to other countries.

This unforgettable trip was my first airplane ride. There were no real seats, but a long bench on two sides of the plane. We sat where the bombs would normally be. I didn't have much time to think as the two Eisner girls and the two Frenchmen all became very ill and I was busy tending them, helping them to the lavatory. I, however, felt wonderful, although very cold.

We flew over Yugoslavia, the Adriatic, and the charming Isle of Albania. Peter and I were invited to come up front with the pilot. The view was breathtaking. Under us, the water was as blue as the sky, like a great mirror, the sail boats like little white points. We were on our way to Bari, the military base for British and Americans in Italy. I wanted the plane to speed up so that I could get there even faster.

In my thoughts and wonderings, I hardly heard our African pilot explaining the wonders of his machine and radio. And then finally we were told to sit down and put our seat belts on. We had arrived at Bari.

I cannot describe the feelings I had. I was overwhelmed with emotion. I could understand the languages being spoken both English and Italian. There would be freedom here. It was truly overwhelming.

After a short customs inspection, we were invited to the British Officers' Mess where the airport personnel, headed by Sergeant Ash, gave us a tea party with <u>real</u> tea and the usual soggy, English ham and cheese sandwiches. For me it was a real treat! To my Balkan heart it was almost too much. If it were not yet complete freedom, it surely was a good beginning and I was young and had so much living yet to do. I accepted every little thing with great humility and happiness.

According to the British Mission, we were to be driven to the city of Bari and put up in a hotel until the Swedes found further assistance in transporting us to Sweden. While we were waiting for a truck to take us into town I had an opportunity to look around. It was the most colorful airport, with the deep blue sky above and thousands of small and large military planes in all colors and shapes. Even the uniforms of the British, American, Italian, Yugoslavian, and Greek soldiers were colorful.

After many "thank-yous" we were put in a

half-open truck and started down a sandy
highway. To me it appeared that we were headed
away from town and not into Bari proper, but
nobody believed this so I shut my mouth and
watched the barren landscape, sure we were going
further and further from the city.

We drove by a colony of tents where Indian
soldiers were living and finally stopped before
our own camp in unforgettable heat. This was
"Transit Camp I," a British camp. As it turned
out it was originally constructed for Jews being
transported out of Italy to the gas chambers.
Now one barracks housed German SS and Gestapo
prisoners under British guard. The other
barracks was for refugees in transit to various
destination countries or enroute to their homes
if they had them. It was also for suspicious
people, which we apparently were thought to be.

We now found out that the fat Englishman
who had stared so suspiciously at me was a
Scotland Yard man. He couldn't figure out why
the German widow of a Swede and I spoke German
instead of Swedish. Also, the Eisner girls spoke
no Swedish. He therefore assumed that we must be
Germans running away, and that perhaps the
Swedes were protecting us for some reason. For
a couple of hours we were put in with some very
suspect people from Italy and Greece.

Later we were placed in fenced-in barracks.
Of course I was furious at the treatment and
demanded to see the Commandant of the camp. Our

older ladies were frightened and tired, so I decided to open my big mouth.

I really shouted and used very angry words at the poor soldier. Finally, when I had to take a breath, he had a chance to explain and tell me that he was sorry but he had no choice. It was Sunday and all the officers were playing cricket. This, of course, made me even angrier. I noticed a big hole in the fence and was ready to step out and go look for the officers myself when the poor soldier picked up his gun and told me, very politely in his cockney English, that he would have to shoot me if I stepped out.

Suddenly, as though I was awakening from a dream, I sat down on the ground, laughing hysterically. How incredibly funny it appeared to me at that moment to be shot by one's ally. I finally stopped laughing. I had my foot back on my side of the fence, and the soldier had his gun at his side, no longer pointing at me. We were both relieved.

As I made peace with the soldier, I looked around. My poor traveling companions looked more than unhappy. It seemed for them that once again this was the end of the world. But at least the English soldier had told me that there was a large stone house on the fenced-in property where we were being kept. It had been a drinking place for the German Cavalry horses. There was lots of cold water, and we could lock it with a big bolt. The soldier was sure that we wouldn't be disturbed by the others in the camp, saying he had never seen anyone else washing among those people. I went immediately to investigate. It was indeed huge and sure enough, had fantastic amounts of cold water, which was a great relief in the extreme heat.

Returning from this little excursion, I found that food had been brought to us by two very unfriendly Yugoslavs, who behaved very badly with my group, except for me. They brought us soup filled with macaroni, meat, tomatoes, and white bread. The soup was in an enormous iron kettle. Nobody but I had an appetite. Like a little pig. I ate so much!

Later, our little English warden brought us chocolate, which everyone ate and enjoyed. Finally, just before it was really dark, an intelligence officer arrived. He told us he was sorry to have to keep us in that place for the night, but our papers weren't in order. First thing, in the morning, he promised we would be okay. I asked him whether he had been playing cricket too, because if he said yes, I might break his neck. As I didn't say it in anger, he smiled and assured me he had not been playing.

There wasn't much to be done in the heat except to go to sleep. We had about twenty beds for only eight of us. Undressing was impossible because it was so dirty. I took a wooden plank out to the backyard to avoid the stuffiness in the barracks, and fell asleep immediately.

It seemed only minutes, but it could have been hours later when I was awakened by screams. I jumped up, ran inside and saw the problem. This time I was not the only naughty one laughing hysterically. There was our very elegant friend, Peter, who always looked as if he had just stepped from a fashion magazine, in his shorts, standing on top of his bed screaming, "Bed bugs! Bed Bugs!" I will never forget that picture. I had great difficulty falling asleep again. None of us could stop laughing.

A bright, sunny, warm Monday morning arrived. After a very cold, but refreshing bath, we were all ready for the interrogations. As I met Peter that morning, I couldn't help but laugh again. I know it wasn't polite, but perhaps the fact that I like to laugh and see the bright side of things is how I have survived all these years.

We were called in one by one. I was questioned about Peter, and he was questioned about me. This was how we discovered that Peter worked for Scotland Yard and now they knew more about me than I myself. The only thing they didn't believe was that I was born a Jew.

Finally they apologized for keeping us, but it seemed there was more to clear up and there were important messages expected to arrive from England and Sweden. We demanded better living conditions so that at least we could sleep in the garden instead of in the insect-ridden building. They gave us blankets and tried to assist us as much as possible.

As Peter and I were the only ones to speak English, we asked permission to go to town, into Bari, and try to get in touch with the Swedish Embassy in Rome. They agreed, but we had to find our own transportation.

So we stood there on the dusty road, and in stages, being picked up by American jeeps or trucks, did get to Bari. The first time an American picked us up, I stood up in the truck like a queen. Of course, I was young, quite attractive with long, clean, reddish-blonde hair and sparkling blue eyes. I almost fell out of the truck in all the excitement. And as Italians passed us, they would shout angrily, "Porco ragazza!" which translates as "piggy girl!' They thought I was an Italian girl flirting with the Americans.

When we first got into Bari we visited the American Military Headquarters. They were surprised and asked if we had been starved or mistreated. We told them no, but it was obvious that the British were not as rich as the Americans.

The beauty of our first day was that besides good sandwiches, Peter and I got a bar of Palmolive soap and two bathrooms with running

hot water and bathtubs. You couldn't imagine
this luxury after what we had been through. We
felt like newborn babies.

In the evening, the Americans drove us back
to the camp with field beds for the ladies. Of
course we were still out in the fenced-in yard,
but the other prisoners were not allowed to come
in. We had special care and by now, of course,
the British and Americans were fighting to treat
us better. After all - we had the wife of a
former Swedish consul, a lady friend of the
Ambassador, the son of a politician and me, who
had worked with Raoul Wallenberg and the Swedish
Red Cross. They fought with each other to take
care of us.

After we got the beds, the British got all
of us more blankets. The Americans got us soup.
The British got us soap. The Americans invited
us to swim in the ocean, dance in their club and
go sailing. The British brought us books to read
and invited us to their library. The Americans
came to visit us in the evenings and many an
evening was spent in quiet talks together with
them and the Scotland Yard people. Naturally we
made many enemies in the camp. We were the
"elite," not refugees.

One day Sergeant Ash came to fetch us to go
to the library and as I was looking for a
suitable book, he pointed to one as the best. I
took it back to camp, and as I browsed through
the pages, I found a 1,000 lira note in it.

First I wondered if someone had left it there by mistake, but slowly I understood that my good friend, Sergeant Ash, had put it there for me. I was embarrassed, but grateful. About a year later, when I was quite secure in Sweden and England was suffering from lack of food, I was happy to be able to send a food parcel to the Ash family. We have remained friends until this day.

We spent all of July in the camp. It took time to investigate our backgrounds and find new transportation to get us to our next stop, Rome. The Swedish Embassy finally found transport for us through the Americans. We got a big military truck with a wonderful sergeant to drive us. The payment for him was three days in Rome. However, one thing was forbidden. There was to be absolutely no alcohol for him.

Once more it was difficult to say good-by to all our military friends on both sides, but we were still anxious to leave. Each of us had someone waiting in Sweden. I was to be married to Toto, and Peter had a wife. I was also looking forward to meeting the Embassy from Budapest, along with Raoul. Little did I know at that time that he would not be coming home with the others.

Our trip took fourteen hours from Bari to Rome and was very tiring and also quite unforgettable. We left very early in the morning. Our first stop was Naples. The truck shook the life out of us, but Judd, our driver, was sure that with his unbelievable voice singing operas and operettas for us, we wouldn't feel it. He was almost entirely right. He sang like Paul Robeson and he never stopped!

In Naples we stopped at a piazza and Judd took out his bottle of soda, wrapped in brown paper. Immediately an MP was there, demanding to see what he was drinking. Judd looked at the man for one second, and then he spit the soda in his face. The M.P. cleaned off his face and left. I wondered, as Judd was a black man, if the M.P. would have questioned him had he been white.

After a short rest, we went on to Capua. Then we were in Monte Casino. Just a short while before, fierce fighting had gone on here, perhaps causing the worst losses of the war. American, Japanese-American, British, Italian and Polish casualties had been enormous. Also the Canadians had suffered great losses here. Rubble and dead animals were everywhere. Yet mimosa trees were in full bloom, the orange trees bore fruit, and oleander trees exhibited their lovely flowers. Nature somehow does not feel pain. Where thousands of young people died, nature came back to give us, the living, beauty and peace. Judd was not singing here. We all prayed.

After we had collected ourselves again, we went on through more rubble, more trees, to

Tivoli. Finally we arrived in the "Eternal City" of Rome, untouched by the war and like a different world.

For me, this was a special arrival. In 1936 I had spent a year in Rome, and I loved every stone, every street corner, every statue. I was supremely grateful that I had survived and could again be in my favorite city.

All the memories of Rome engulfed me. Later, we settled in the little hotel nicely reserved for us by the Swedish Embassy. They also supplied us with enough money to get through our stay in Rome. Naturally all of us had to return this money after our arrival in Sweden. In my case, my fiance was going to repay it.

I was reminded of my stay in Rome in 1936, when I took a course with Madame Montessori herself, learning how to handle emotionally disturbed children. It was a fascinating course, and I earned a diploma as a Montessori teacher. In the time when I had no studies, I had roamed the museums and had gone to many concerts. I had met an Italian officer who wore a monocle. Frankly, today, I don't know if I was in love with the man, or his great uniform and monocle. The fact was that he loved me and we had wanted to get married. He was looking for a Military Attache job, preferably in Budapest.

While I had gone home to prepare for the wedding, it happened that he had a child by an Italian woman. It was either marry her and have a career or marry me and lose the career. He chose the former. I corresponded with his family until war broke out and now, in 1945, it was a pleasure to see them again. They told me that my former fiance had married the girl, but was never happy. For my part, I was young enough to be hurt, but also young enough to forget the pain.

Strangely enough, the second time I fell in love it was once again with an Italian, but he was forbidden to me as he was married. Then I was older and in Budapest, where morals were very strict. That time it was more difficult to handle my emotions. As I was now in Rome, I tried to find him and his family, but I could not. Only much later, when I was in Stockholm, did I discover their whereabouts.

In Rome we had lots of surprises. Our English friends, including Sergeant Ash, took a well deserved vacation and joined us for a week. We went to hear Benjamina Gigli and Toti Dal Monte in Mascagni's Cavalleria Rusticana, performed in a wide open arena. It was a fabulous performance, particularly if you only listened, as both of them were very fat. When they wanted to kiss, they couldn't because of their fat bellies. But this was minor considering their magnificent voices. We were so hungry for good music.

Finding Gigli alive was a great surprise for me. Just before I left Budapest, during my good-bys to my mother, we were listening to a recording of Gigli singing his famous song, "Mama." It was very emotional. Shortly thereafter the BBC announced that he had died. When I arrived in Rome and saw a big placard announcing the forthcoming opera I couldn't believe my eyes. I went to a music store and asked and found out happily that he was indeed still alive. Their performance was one of those highlights of my life, like coming out of a long coma and learning about life again, seeing happy faces, hearing music that went right to my heart and having friends to enjoy such a precious moment with me.

We had almost a month's stay in Rome. I made sure that I revisited all the corners of this great city again. I went to stand and speak quietly with my favorite - Michaelangelo's "Moses", housed in a beautiful church called San Pietro di Vincoli.

In Rome, as elsewhere in Italy, there is siesta time. Churches and museums close at noon and reopen at 2:00 p.m. I made it my business to be there on the dot of 2:00 so I could have some time alone. When you stand there before this marble wonder, you feel it is alive! His face is full of vitality and spirit. One feels love and terror at the same time. One finds peace and somehow answers to questions. In the frame of mind in which I had been, this was the greatest strength I received. It renewed my soul.

From there I went to St. Peter's Basilica and stood before Michaelangelo's "Pieta." The silence and serenity made me realize that I had received all the blessings of the world. What a gift to be allowed to take in all this beauty when so many millions had perished. I was a very lucky young woman.

Then I went to the Villa Borghese and walked around in the magnificent gardens. I went to the top of the "Pincho," a terrace overlooking all of Rome. Besides the magnificent view there was a little stand. Here a man put delicious Italian bread with proscuitto ham and cheese in a little oven and served it with delicious vermouth. It topped off the incredible day.

During this time I also wrote of my adventures to my parents. Our English friends, Sergeant Ash and the others, had good connections with the Red Cross and through them, every week a letter could be sent from me to Budapest. I was almost the only one who had left Hungary at that time, so my letters went into some of the Hungarian papers so that the people were informed of what was happening in the world outside. That was at the beginning. Later, they could not publish anything from outside.

One afternoon in Rome we walked on the Via
Veneto with the two Eisner girls with whom I had
traveled. We were minding our own business when
a big American car came by and the officers in
it tried to pick us up. They spoke in Italian
of course. We just lifted our heads and
pretended we could not hear them, so they tried
in English. This didn't work either, so after a
while I turned my head and proudly said that we
were Swedish. The car door opened and a very
good looking, tall blonde chap jumped out. He
happily told us that he was a Swedish-American
from Minneapolis and merrily began to speak
Swedish. At this point I had to laugh and I
explained to him who we were. He was amused but
disappointed and went back to the car and drove
off.

At the end of August, with the help of the
British Mission, we got a private bus and
started our long, eighteen hour trip, through
Rieti, Spaleto, Assissi, Peruggia, Florence,
Parma, Milano and Como to Chiasso, where we
entered Switzerland.

This was another emotional point in our
journey. I had many relatives in this country,
whom I called at once. My mother's sister was
there with her family. I slept almost all the
way to Zurich. When we arrived there in the
morning, my family was waiting for me. It was a
wonderful moment after so long.

This was truly a country without the

ravages of war, a country at peace. Going through the streets, it seemed strange not to see military trucks and uniforms. It was really freedom! I don't think anyone who hasn't gone through war can understand this feeling. My family understood, but speaking with others who had spent the war in Switzerland, they couldn't believe me.

I tried to explain what had happened and how people had been saved by Raoul Wallenberg, but other than my family, nobody seemed even interested in the stories. I was disappointed in them for not listening because I felt it so important, and after a short while I stopped talking. Perhaps if I had not stopped, Raoul would be with us today, instead of in a Russian Gulag.

Almost a whole month was spent in Zurich, which I thoroughly enjoyed. I renewed my acquaintance with my dear aunt, Irma, who still today, at age 90, is a very well know pianist. I also got to know my late uncle Sasha, who was a great conductor and violinist. He was originally from Odessa, Russia. It was marvelous to hear music in their home and I enjoyed the company of my cousins again. I took time out one day to visit our old family friends in Geneva. That turned out to be a disappointment. The valued possessions we had left with them for safe keeping had all disappeared. When we finally left for Sweden, I didn't even have a warm coat to take with me.

Back in Rumania I had had a very good fur coat, but a dear friend of mine had been attacked by Russian soldiers. She was very ill and had no money, so I paid for the doctor for her with my fur. She got well and today, forty years later, is a happy mother in Israel.

From our original Swedish group only three of us were left in Zurich: the lady who got me in trouble because we spoke German on the airplane after we left Bucharest, Imre, a Hungarian man married to a Swedish girl, and myself. The Swedish lady, Mr. Danielson's Hungarian lady friend, the Eisner girls and Peter had been flown to Stockholm earlier.

Finally, at the end of September, we got our "marching orders" and readied ourselves for our departure. We became members of a convoy arranged by the Norwegian Army Transport Service in Switzerland and the Norwegian Military Mission in Germany.

CHAPTER 5

Just before our trip on the Red Cross Convoy, I spent some time with my friend's husband from Geneva. He was a journalist for the Swedish Aftonbladet and I was the first arrival from the war zone. The war was over in May and this was September. I told him the story of Raoul and thanked the Swedish government and the Legation of Budapest for their great effort in saving so many people. I told him that there was a song written to Raoul although it was since lost. He was fascinated by the incredible story and of course put some of his own imagination into his article. But I found this out only later when I realized that things had not gone the way they should have.

A day after my interview with my friend we were ready to leave with the Red Cross. The passengers were composed of Norwegians, Danes, Dutch and Swedes who were caught in Switzerland for the duration of the war. There were also three of us from the original eight who were flown to Sweden before this time. The drivers were German war prisoners, each with a swastika hanging in front of them.

As we lined up for the departure, the Swiss authorities took all the food and money from everyone. True, Switzerland was still on rationing, but actually they didn't want for anything and they must have known that our trip through Germany would take days. There would be no food there, not even for money.

As I was almost at the end of the line, I went into the bathroom and put the little money I had in my shoe and walked out again. I couldn't face not having any money, even if we couldn't buy anything in Germany. I would at least need it in Denmark and Sweden. I was asked by one of the Norwegians if I could speak German, because they were fluent in that language but did not want to talk to the Germans. I was therefore, unfortunately, designated to sit with the first bus driver and give him instructions since I understood the signs on the roads and bridges which were all written in English. I had to sit with this Nazi for three days. This was essential, as there were so many places where signs announced "Watch out - no bridge" or "no road." It was tiresome and unpleasant, but I had no choice, and at least I knew it would come to an end.

We traveled from Basel through Freiburg, Karlsruhe, Heidelberg, Mannheim, Darmstadt, and Hanau to Frankfurt am Mein, where we had a rest for the night in a bombed out house. Of course we were not supposed to go out , but I did, with a Danish man. There was so much sickness and still some corpses lying about, we went to see the damage. Along the way we saw long lines of German war prisoners being escorted by British or American troops. I wanted to feel some sorrow or compassion, but could not do it. I

94

kept remembering the stories I had heard from
some of the survivors of the camps, even though
at that time I was unaware of the vast numbers
of people killed there. Any sympathy I might
have had vanished. I was grateful that the
three drivers of our busses did not want to
commit suicide with us in the bus. They were
quite arrogant and still tried to act superior.
But they took my directions well for all that.
I imagine they knew that there was much danger
on the road. Besides, there were really no Jews
on the bus to their knowledge. It would have
been amusing had they known their orders were
coming from a Jew!

After we left Frankfurt am Mein, we went on
with few stops through Menningen, Kassel,
Hanover, Hamburg, Lubeck, New Munster, Kiel,
Schleswig and finally, after three days, the
Danish border town of Flensburg. What awaited
us in Flensburg was again unbelievable. The
Danes had a village with barracks waiting for
us. It was very modern with hot showers the
likes of which we hadn't seen before. There
were dining rooms with food piled up. To us it
looked like enough for two full armies to feast
upon. The wonderful people of Denmark couldn't
do enough to make us comfortable.

So many Jews had been saved by the Danes.
There is now a museum there dealing with the
Danish resistance to the Nazis. They continued
throughout the war to actively resist the Nazis
and support their Jewish citizens.

The story of how the King insisted on wearing a yellow armband is well known but what is less know is how non-Jewish neighbors maintained the gardens and homes of Danish Jews until their return from involuntary exile. Danes also left their jobs and joined a secret Navy working with the British in the Caribbean against the Nazi submarines there. The Danes are an incredible people.

After enjoying their hospitality, we were driven through Korsor and Kalendborg to Copenhagen and were shown a little of this great city. Then, finally, we went to Helsingor, the little fishing village from which the Danes had a ferry system to take Danish Jews at night over to Helsingborg in Sweden where they lived out the war. The two countries had managed this beautifully throughout the duration.

The three of us then took a ferry way over to Helsingborg. When we arrived there, we had our first disappointment in a long time. As it turned out, my passport was not good for Sweden. I tried to explain as best I could, that other countries had let me come in even Switzerland because it was a Swedish passport, but it was no good. We were told that my two traveling companions could get in, but not me. They had received no prior information about our coming. As my two dear friends would not abandon me, the police decided to let all three of us in and took us to a little Swedish pensione to sleep.

In the morning at eight o'clock, there was
a knock at the door. It was the same two
detectives from the night before. This time
they were smiling and inviting us out for
breakfast. And a great breakfast it was! After
that, they took me to the police station where I
met the Police Chief. If my memory serves me
correctly, his name was Johnson. He was tall,
blue-eyed, blond, middle aged. He could not
speak English, but he spoke some German. He
took me in his arms and cried. I was surprised.
I had no idea why he was crying. Then he shoved
a newspaper into my hands. I couldn't read
Swedish, so he explained, in his limited German,
that the article covered an interview I had
given in Geneva. This article had preceded me on
September 5, 1945, about a week before my
arrival. During the night they had called the
Foreign Office in Stockholm to verify my
identity. They were told to let me free at once
and to give me money so that I could reach my
destination.

My dear friends left on the first train to
Stockholm after giving me their phone numbers so
that I could call them on my own arrival.

Chief Johnson then asked if I wanted to go
to Stockholm or Orebro, the birthplace of my
fiance. I decided to go to Orebro to my future
mother-in-law. Chief Johnson must have notified
her of my arrival because she was at the railway
station. I spoke no Swedish and she no English,
but that didn't seem to matter. We liked each

97

other at once, and love knows no barriers. She was a lovely lady. She took me to her hair dresser and had a copy of the newspaper article with her. With a big smile she explained to everyone that Toto, my fiance, was in Stockholm and that the two of us were going to see him on the weekend.

The train to Stockholm was so very comfortable, and Mrs. Hallberg of course took the article with her on the train and told everyone about it. All the people gave me welcoming smiles and all I could say, as in Bucharest was "tack so mycket" (thank you).

On our arrival in Stockholm, it was already evening. There was the man I was to marry - the man who had really saved my life. There was Toto in the flesh, with another man. Instead of a hug I got a greeting of a clenched fist from both of them. I was so shocked by it that I had to ask what kind of greeting it was. Toto said, "Communist, of course." I froze. I was thinking that it was just a tasteless joke, not real, and that after a good night's sleep the bad feeling would disappear. But it stayed on late in the evening as we all went to the boarding house Toto had reserved for us.

A pleasant man opened the door and said that as we were late he had rented the room already. My fiance did not offer to help us look for other lodgings. As a matter of fact, he and his friend were in a great rush to go to a meeting. He gave us a phone number where we could reach him in the morning and turned and left.

This was the second disappointment since my arrival. It was already after ten o'clock and I couldn't call anyone for help, so Toto's mother and I walked half the night until finally we found a small hotel that had a room for us. We washed, hugged and went to sleep immediately.

In the morning it was sunny but quite cold. We dressed and made a call to Toto. He picked us up. We walked around Stockholm, had lunch and then walked his mother back to the railway station. I have never seen her again, but I know that she too could not understand the behavior of her son.

After that Toto walked with me back to the hotel and I found out why the other man had met me yesterday. Evidently my journalist friend in Geneva had drawn his own conclusions about my travels. Instead of ending my trip the way I explained it, he wrote that I had come on a mission to Sweden and was going on to Oslo, Norway. So Toto and his friend were sure that I was a communist and that the government in Hungary had sent me on some mission to Scandinavia. This baffled me. I couldn't understand why Toto would be interested in that. As he again was in a hurry, there was no time to ask him. All I could tell him was how very thankful my family and I were that he had saved

our lives. Neither of us mentioned a word about
an upcoming marriage. I went upstairs and, for
the first time since my arrival, had a good cry.

The next morning was again sunny. I was not
in the best of spirits and it was bitterly cold,
and I was without a winter coat. The concierge
was very kind and made a call for me to the
Swedish Foreign Department so that I could make
an appointment with Minister Danielson. I was
told to come immediately to see him and the rest
of the Legation.

What a great reunion it was! Minister
Danielson, Per Anger, Mr. Mezey. In a few
minutes I discovered the terrible truth about
Raoul, that he was not back in Sweden, and that
his mother had received a call from the Russian
Ambassador saying that he had been in protective
custody since the previous January. Everyone
was hoping for his speedy return.

They told me about their long eight day trip
from Ploesty to Moscow in the comfortable but
strictly curtained cars. They were never
allowed off the train, or even to look out.
They had plenty of vodka and caviar, but no
freedom whatsoever. When they had arrived in
Moscow, the Swedish Ambassador to Russia had
told them not to make any inquires about Raoul.
They didn't understand his request but they had
to oblige.

If all of us had listened to our instincts

instead of what officials told us to do, we would have spoken up for our friend instead of being docile. Perhaps he would now be with us instead of having spent over forty years in Russian captivity, suffering, while we have a good life.

But there we were, October, 1945, all of us in Sweden. I told them my story and how I arrived. I also had to tell them of my strange meeting with my fiance and his friend. They too had read the Aftonbladet article and couldn't understand why I would want to go to Oslo. After I explained the misinterpretation they were happy. I thanked them all for what they had done and we all spoke lovingly about Raoul.

I asked them if it was possible to find out if my fiance and his friend were communists. I was concerned as that would put me in a very delicate position. I wanted them to understand that I could not marry a man like that.

They said that perhaps there would be an answer to this the next day as the Communist party sat in the Swedish parliament and there was a list of names of communists.

I thanked them for everything once again, and they gave me money to live for a few days. I took my leave and went in search of my traveling companions. Imre was reunited with his wife and very happy. Peter was also with his wife and had a job that appeared to be

connected with Scotland Yard. The Eisner girls
were with their parents, my German friend was
with her Swedish family, and the other lady was
well too. The only one not so fortunate was the
Hungarian friend of the Ambassador. She was in
a sanatorium with tuberculosis. I visited her
immediately. She was so happy to see me again.
She looked so healthy. She had put on weight
and had very rosy cheeks. I was sure she would
be out soon. Instead she was dead in a few
months. Here was a girl, an aristocrat from
Hungary, who was also against the Nazis. She
had survived all the horrors of the war and now,
in great safety, she had to die. My heart was
very heavy and full of sorrow when I heard of
her death.

I also met Ilse again. She was the one who
was hidden in the Legation with her two sons.
She left Hungary with Per Anger on almost the
last train. It was wonderful to know that I
wasn't alone. I didn't feel so miserable.

In two days, Mr. Mezey called me to the
office. Yes, I was right. Toto and the man
with him were members of the Communist Party in
Stockholm. Toto's friend, in fact, was the
leader of the Stockholm Communist Party. He
said I wasn't obliged to marry him, but it was
my responsibility to repay to the Swedish
government all the money I had spent during
those long months. I said that hopefully I
would be able to do this, but after many years
of trying unsuccessfully, I finally received an

official letter from the Swedish government saying that I didn't need to repay the money. I have never found a way to show my gratitude to the Swedes for their generosity. Perhaps one day when this book is published I will be able to show how much I love and respect them.

Mr. Danielson told me that the Hungarian Embassy would have a job waiting for me. I was frightened to go there, but Mr. Danielson assured me that someone would wait outside and if I didn't return in an hour they would come for me.

With this encouragement, I went to the Hungarian Embassy. My heart was in my mouth. I met the Vice Counsul, whose name I don't recall. He was very nice, asked if I needed anything, offered me coffee and was generally very pleasant. Then he told me about the job. It was the greatest job offer I had ever had! He said that the Hungarian Government wanted me as their Cultural Attache in Stockholm. I was speechless. I couldn't believe what I was hearing. My mind was jumping. What a great honor! What a wonderful job! What a new life for me...and what a fool I would be if I did work for the new government, never mind how fantastic the job.

Turning to him and saying "Thank you, but no thank you," was one of the most difficult things I have had to do. I explained to him that I could not work for the new Hungarian

government. He said he understood and shook my
hand. I left quickly. In a couple of weeks I
heard that he had asked for political asylum in
Sweden. That explained why he understood my
feelings so quickly.

Then, almost immediately, a new job came on
the horizon. It was certainly time for it. The
weather was colder and I had to get a fur coat
in a hurry. I wrote a letter to Geneva to ask
my friends if they could spare funds for a coat,
but the answer was "Agi, you are such an able
person. You will create the money to buy your
coat." They were right. I got my coat, but not
before I got the worst cold of my life.

Count Bernadotte brought survivors from all
camps into Sweden and opened the finest health
facilities for those who were ill. They were
old military facilities, hotels, and sanatoriums
remodeled and fully staffed with doctors,
nurses. Food, clothing and other necessities
were made available.

Count Bernadotte, just like Raoul, was a
great humanitarian and could not stand the
suffering of others. Unfortunately, he was
killed in error in Palestine shortly after he
brought these people to Sweden.

The Swedish Government in cooperation with
Swenska Institutet (Swedish Institute) was
looking for people with a good knowledge of
Sweden and Swedish literature to go and speak to

these people in their own languages, which in this case were Hungarian, German, French, and Polish. I spoke the first three languages.

The Swenska Institutet is an institute for exchange of foreign students, and now wholeheartedly wished to help these sick people. They gave me a key to the Royal Library where I could find books written in German, about the history of Sweden, about their music, and about famous writers like Selma Lagerlof and Stendahl.

My job was to explain the culture of Sweden to these people, to let them know about the life of their host country. I also asked permission to speak about Raoul Wallenberg to the Hungarians. I felt that perhaps some of their families had survived because of him and it was important for them to know that there was somebody out there who cared a lot.

It was a fascinating job. I traveled first class on trains everywhere. That was how I learned to speak Swedish. It was wonderful knowing the language rather than just the few words I knew back in Bucharest. Sometimes I learned the hard way. One day as it happened, I was on a train at lunch time and we were almost at my destination. We had just finished lunch and the waiter, whom I knew from an earlier trip, asked me if I wanted "Judgubbar" for dessert. As I am not a great dessert eater, I said no, but he looked at me very puzzled and repeated, "No Judgubbar". I said "No, thack so mycket," and he shrugged his shoulders and left. In a minute he returned and brought my companions the freshest, most wonderful strawberries with cream. I looked at them with amazement. "Judgubbar?" He smiled at me and I watched sorrowfully as my companions ate the wonderful strawberries. Surely I never forgot that word. And the next time I traveled on that train with the same waiter, he simply smiled and arrived with my "Judgubbar" at the end of my meal.

On another trip my train arrived late for a connection and the good people at the railway station let me board a freight train. It was an open car with heavy logs on top. I joined a group of lumberjacks and sat with them. We traveled through an incredibly beautiful countryside. We tried to make conversation and sang beautiful Swedish songs. This is the way to learn a language. They were rugged, wonderful people.

Another memorable trip was to a far away camp in mid-winter when the snows were very heavy. A big limousine picked me up at the train station and the driver asked me if I liked classical music. I asked why and he said that Beethoven's 9th Symphony was coming and our trip would last as long as the symphony. I was thrilled. Imagine a moonlit night with heavy snow, driving through the snow laden trees with the most fantastic music and singing as company. Just pine trees, snow and glorious music. Again

I felt humbled by the wonderful rewards I was receiving.

The camps themselves were an experience. One would think that all the horrors these people experienced would kill their love of beauty, but no. We are amazing creatures. In one of the camps was a dear Polish man, perhaps in his early 20's. He didn't talk much, but after listening to some of Selma Lagerlof's best stories, he asked me if I wanted to listen to some Heine poems in German. To my amazement this man, who had suffered so much and lost all his family, sat and recited, without error, these powerful poems.

I once again reminded myself of the importance Raoul had placed on saving the young. There must be thousands of young around the world whose lives were touched by Raoul Wallenberg one way or another and they, just like this wonderful young Polish man, would give pleasure to others. I learned from each of these experiences and hopefully grew with each of them.

In the meantime, the Swenska Institutet gave me a charming partner who came along with film equipment and movies of Sweden. This was not only good for the people in the camps, but it also gave me a new friend. He was a funny human being with a dear wife and children who all became my friends. Swen had a car, so I seldom traveled by train after that.

107

I never knew before that I could be a public speaker. I was an only child, and had not much opportunity to give speeches. I was surprised to see that sometimes a very difficult audience was spellbound by some of the stories I told them.

One day, one of my superiors decided to come to one of the camps with Swen and myself and listen to my stories. Usually I was told to limit the stories to a half hour. This time, of course, I was worried whether my boss would approve of my presentation. It really did not help that my dear friend Swen stood outside the window making faces at me. It was difficult not to burst out laughing. But as soon as I started to tell a story I was in a different world of make believe. Automatically I tried to act the story out as best I could. When I finished my half hour, I came back to reality. It was very quiet and my boss said, "Can you tell another story?" Of course I agreed and spoke for another half hour with the audience still in rapt attention.

It was a great success and yet a month later I was called to the office at the Swenska Institutet and told that I would not be able to go to the camps for a while as some of the Hungarian inmates had complained of my anti-Communist speeches. I couldn't figure this out as I was telling them stories from the Swedish books and Swen was showing them films. Often, however, after the stories, some of the

108

Hungarien people would ask if I had any news
from Hungary. They wondered if they should go
home. I could only tell them what I had heard
from my parents - that it was very difficult at
the moment with food shortages, no medicine,
etc.   I tried to explain that perhaps they
should wait a while.   I told them that the
Swedish government was taking such good care of
them, tending to their illnesses, giving them
clothing, medication, and love.

     I asked my boss if this could be construed
as an anti-communist speech. He couldn't reply
until all the camp directors had been contacted.

     I therefore was out of work.   This was a
big blow as I still had to pay for lodging and
food.   I got myself a job in a factory making
curtain rods.   It was piece work and as I am not
very handy, it was slow and my fingers were cut
to ribbons.   There were days when I stood crying
at my window looking down at the street where a
vendor sold delicious frankfurters for 25 ore,
which I could not afford.

     This deprivation also passed.   I got the
call which informed me that all camp directors
agreed with my story. They apologized and
backpaid me for the month and I happily resumed
my original job.

     However, within six months, the job ceased
as the patients got well and were able to go
back to their countries or to Israel and

America. Some of them married Swedes or simply decided to stay.

In the meantime I found an apartment to share with a woman and also got a job as a maid in a very good hotel. One of my knees swelled, but it was interesting work and paid well. After a week they asked me to become a supervisor but I preferred my work as a maid. It was interesting to note that every room had a Russian book of some sort. Everybody was learning Russian.

Now I understood why they had been so concerned about my speeches in the camps. This frightened me. I feared that the Russians would come and then where would I go? I was happy in Sweden, and the thought of moving again was not good.

I also met Toto a couple of times, but this friendship didn't go anywhere. I knew and he knew that there would be no marriage. He finally told me that he had fallen in love with some other girl, although his mother was very fond of me. We eventually parted friends. There were certainly no hard feelings on my side. After all, he had saved my life.

Then, as always, a miracle happened again. One Sunday afternoon I was alone in the apartment, soaking my swollen knee, when the telephone rang. At first I wasn't going to answer it, but some instinct made me pick it up.

It was the Director of Skandinaviska Banken. He
told me that they had a job for me and asked if
I could come in on Monday. I could only mutter
"thank you" and hung up screaming with
excitement. I immediately called the hotel and
told them I would not be in the following day.

Next morning I arrived at nine o'clock at
this very beautiful bank. I was hired in the
foreign check department as of that day. The
salary was very good. I was taken around to
meet other employees and everyone spoke English.
All were very pleasant to me. I was taken to
lunch in the employees lunchroom on the top
floor of the bank where we were served by
waitresses. It was again like a dream.

I made friends very quickly. Everybody was
glad to speak English, and I was happy to speak
Swedish. I learned quite fast what I was to do
in the department and every day it was fun to
come to work. I was suddenly a "lady" again. I
had friends, food, clothing, and could write
regularly to my parents and receive mail.

With my first paycheck I sent a package to
my parents and the family of Sergeant Ash in
England. I also began to look for an apartment,
which was not easy in Stockholm.

I rented one furnished from the daughter of
the Director of the bank. She had had a baby and
had left her apartment for a few months. It was
in a very good neighborhood in a big complex.

111

It had wonderful facilities for working parents with a baby nursery in the house and a regular nursery and kindergarten. It also had a restaurant so that the parents could leave the children in good hands and come home and have dinner before picking up the children.

This is such an incredible convenience. I have often wondered why the United States and other countries don't have the same facilities.

After the girl returned with her baby, I found a nice, one-room apartment for a year. It belonged to a friend of mine who had gone to the States. It was unfurnished, but lovely. I slept on the floor one night and went to work happily. When I came home in the afternoon I proudly looked up at my windows and was very surprised to find curtains hanging. I thought perhaps it was not my window after all. I ran up quickly and opened the door and just stood there. Indeed there were curtains on the windows, flowers, a mattress on the floor in the living room, tables, chairs in the kitchen. There was everything you could think of - even a broom and pail.

The next day when I went to the office everyone hugged me and asked me if I liked it? I was ecstatic and wondered how they had done it.

They explained that there were VIP rooms in the bank. Whenever they had foreign visitors they didn't have to go to a hotel, but were put up in the bank itself. There was a huge storage area in the basement with things they hadn't used for years. Two of my colleagues and two of the porters asked one of the directors for permission to use the things to furnish my apartment. They loaded it all on a truck, had the super open my apartment and fixed it up for me. I felt very humble and happy!

As is the custom in Sweden, I had a specific day that was my own for doing laundry and had access to a vacuum cleaner and floor waxer. Although it was many years after that that I became involved with Japanese customs, I insisted already that everyone should take off their shoes when they came in.

During this time my parents came to visit. My father came on a mission to get money to build up the Protestant churches in Budapest. My parents were both very active in trying to save people and much had been lost during the bombing of the city. I asked them to stay in Stockholm but they felt conditions would improve in Hungary and that they should return.

I was not happy to see them go back, but I understood that it must be much more difficult for older people to leave their homeland permanently. Finally, just before the "curtain" went down on Hungary, they got out, and had to come back to Sweden.

In the meantime my life continued to improve. I loved my adopted country. I wrote many poems. I was elected to the International Club, which was for artists and writers. I was really honored. We had a good social life in the bank too, with Christmas parties and New Year's balls. I also went to concerts as often as possible, as I could get tickets through a new friend who worked in the theatre office of the department store called Nordiska Companiet.

What I didn't do, however, was, to get in touch with the Wallenberg family. I so much wanted to see Raoul's mother and tell her about her lovely son. However I felt it might be an imposition, that they might think I wanted something from them. Today, I am so sorry to have missed many years of Raoul's sister, Nina's, friendship, as I very much admire her. I am happy that today I can be her friend, after so many years were wasted.

Life continued, but there was unrest everywhere and the feeling that the Soviets wanted more territory. Many people were thinking that Sweden would be their next target. I didn't want to hear that. I was too happy and satisfied, but somehow in the back of my mind was a constant nagging. Somehow I knew I had to get out of Europe. I couldn't explain the feeling because I really was happy. I had a good and free life that I had always dreamed of, a circle of friends I was proud of, but the nagging did not stop. I finally went to the

U.S. Embassy and asked if I could emigrate. I was told that the Hungarian quota was filled at that time, but they accepted my papers.

It was a difficult decision. I couldn't have asked for a finer country or people nicer than the Swedes. I felt as if I had always lived there, belonged there. In Sweden when you make a friend you have a friend for life. I didn't mind the cold climate as everyone I met was smiling and warm. I had all the reasons in the world to want to become a proud Swede. I had written more poems than ever. I had wonderful discussions in the evenings with friends. I learned Swedish, and my friends learned English. I corresponded with my parents and asked them to please join me in Stockholm. Life was so beautiful and yet the nagging continued. The news was fearful. I was restless and afraid of the unknown. I was also very discouraged that Raoul had not returned and I kept thinking of leaving Europe.

In the meantime, my parents got their visa to come to Stockholm. Aunt Rosa and Lydia were ready to leave for an American camp in Germany arranged by Aunt Rosa's brother who was in the American army. Anita and Zoltan had a baby and they stayed in Budapest. I also picked up correspondence with good friends of ours in Sydney, Australia. I was told emigration to Australia was easy and that they were willing to sponsor me. And there went the life of beauty I was unwilling to give up. It was hard to explain why I felt I had to leave.

By the sixth of February, 1948, I got my emigration visa from the Australian Embassy. I went to the American Embassy to have my future emigration to the States forwarded to Sydney. My parents arrived and we got a temporary apartment. Papa got a good job where he didn't have to speak Swedish. Even in 1948, the Swedes did all they could for people who had to live in their homeland. It was not an easy time for me to pack up again and start a new life when I could have become a Swedish citizen in a very short while. I would have been proud of that, and it seemed even the Swedish government did not want to see me go. As always they understood my fears and uneasiness. They even helped me with financing my trip to Australia. No wonder that Sweden produces men like Raoul Wallenberg. Under that cold, Nordic beauty, there is such a great heart and understanding. It was the first time in my life that I felt equal to anyone. I felt very much a Swede, and I feel even today that it could have been the country of my birth rather than the Hungary I left in such a hurry.

There I was. My parents had barely arrived and I was leaving with the dream that maybe in Australia I would find a good job and become rich. Perhaps I could finally be able to bring my parents out and we could all live together in peace again. I booked passage on a cargo boat, the Wangaratta, which would take twelve passengers only. The trip would be five weeks and I had to travel to Oslo, Norway to board the ship.

The weeks before my departure were filled with emotion. Once again there were the rounds of sad good-bys from friends at the bank, at the Foreign Ministry, and others I had met. I went all by myself to all the beautiful places I often walked. Finally I had to say good-by to my parents again. I knew they would be all right, and yet it was not an easy thing to leave them there alone. My friends all promised to look after them as they would look after their own parents, and they did as they promised.

Finally the day of my departure arrived and I had to take the night train to Oslo as we had to register on the ship by four the next afternoon. Needless to say I cried most of the night to Oslo. There went my life, my parents, my friends, and my hope to have seen Raoul again.

Suddenly I was no longer a Swedish citizen. I traveled on an alien passport into the unknown world of a country I knew so little about. But my optimism won out after all. I was going to make that new life at least half as good as it was in my beloved Sweden. So I dried my tears and looked forward to my arrival in Oslo.

CHAPTER 6

It was early morning, around seven, when I arrived at the station in Oslo. It was sunny and cold on that April 10th. I took a cab to the pier and there stood the beautiful ship. I was escorted onto the boat and was shown to my state room. It was big and lovely with a little living area and bedroom and a very big bathroom with four different faucets - two regular water, warm and cold, and two sea-water faucets. I was told that I would be seated at the captain's table with a Swedish baroness and her 12-year-old son. I was to be back aboard by four that afternoon. It all sounded quite wonderful and I went off to see Oslo.

I was back before four and unpacked. They I went to explore the ship. The kitchen was a great surprise. Everything was made fresh, all the pastries, salads, meats, and fish. The staff was busy getting ready for our first meal. The deck was clean and comfortable. There was a large living room with armchairs, tables, games, card tables, flowers, books and magazines. Altogether it was very comfortable and luxurious.

At six o'clock a bell rang. This was the departure bell. It was very exciting as we pulled away from the pier. In a short while, Oslo looked like a tiny toy city, and I was crying again, wholeheartedly. I felt like jumping off and swimming back to Sweden. But it was too late!

At seven the bell rang again. This time it was ringing for dinner. As I arrived in the dining room, I was immediately taken to the captain's table, and introduced to this charming, warm man, and to my companions, the baroness and her charming 12 year old son, with whom I immediately made friends.

The trip was quite exciting. We passed by the Danish shores, then the French shores to Spain and the Canary Islands. This was our first and only stop for fresh food and fuel. The Captain invited the baroness, her little boy and myself to the restaurant owned by the man who supplied the food for the ship. It was on the top of the island. We went by car up a winding, very flowery road, and always we could see the beauty of the Atlantic Ocean below us as we went further up. It was a very pleasant trip and at lunch I had the finest grilled shrimp I have ever eaten, topped off by fine Spanish wines.

We came down from there in a happy mood. After we had returned to the boat, there was a knock on my cabin door. I opened it to see the biggest flower arrangement I had ever seen. It took two men to bring it in, and it had the most foul smell I had ever smelled. The captain came in laughing. We had to put it in the bathtub. He then explained what the foul smell was. Somehow the flowers on this beautiful island have no smell, and as the owner of the restaurant had wanted very much to please me, he put a certain oil on the flowers to give them a scent.

No matter how much water we used to rinse the flowers, we couldn't get the smell off. Nothing helped, so after a few hours out at sea, we ceremoniously threw all of them into the ocean. But the captain was very pleased at my great success with the restaurant owner. They kidded me about it for weeks. The captain also showed me his very wonderful lodging on deck, where he had exotic plants and flowers with delightful scents! This was one of the captain's hobbies. He had his walls lined with great books and gave me permission to take any I wanted to read. He was like a good father to me. It was a great comfort.

The food on the ship was superb, and it was quite a smooth journey until we neared Africa. There we had rough seas and everyone was sick except the boy and I. We still sat there proudly and played checkers. Neither of us had the guts to tell the other the inevitable. Finally he got up and told me he had to look for something. I smiled, and as soon as he was out of sight, I ran like mad to my bathroom. In a few minutes a messenger arrived from the captain. He asked me to be on deck in a minute. In a wailing voice I said I couldn't make it. The messenger told me that it was an order and nobody dared say "no." I was so distressed that

I followed him up on deck where the captain stood laughing.

He told me to look out to sea and if I had to, to give it to the fishes. I gulped a few times, trying to be very brave. I inhaled the salty air, looked at the frightening gray waves coming over the deck and shaking the whole boat. Then, miraculously, my stomach stopped going around and I could breathe freely. All sickness seemed to disappear. The captain took my hands and said that the best way not to get seasick was to be up there looking at the angry sea. He was absolutely right, of course. Downstairs the smell of food and lack of ventilation were the reasons you stayed sick, and, truly, I was not sick again.

The seas calmed as we drew closer to the African coast, Cape Verde and Dakar. We then reached the Equator and the Captain wanted a great celebration. First he put up a heavy canvas plank and filled it with sea water. We were oiled and ducked in this water with great shrieks of laughter. Then, in the evening, we had a formal dinner party. It is lovely when you are young, because you are still full of vanity, and I certainly was, that night! I had a great white evening gown, and by now I was nicely sun kissed. My golden reddish blond hair was gleaming and clean. I had the naughtiness to arrive in the dining room last so that everybody had to notice me. The captain asked if I had just come from a Paris beauty salon. I was a fresh kid then, but it was wonderful to be noticed. Maybe this is just human, but sometimes I feel that you go through life like a little point with nobody knowing that you are alive, and life is too short. At that very moment we were at the Equator and I wanted to be noticed. I certainly succeeded!

As we sailed into the Indian Ocean, it was warm and beautiful. Thanks to our lovely captain, we could plunge into his improvised little canvas pool and refresh ourselves.

We passed Capstad and Port Elizabeth and finally, on May 23, 1948, we arrived in Melbourne, Australia. The captain told me he would bring my luggage the following week to Sydney, as it would have cost a fortune to send it by plane.

My arrival in Melbourne was not so pleasant because the customs officer made me very angry. I had purchased two little plastic handbags for the two little girls I would see in Sydney at a shop in Stockholm. They wanted to charge me three pounds duty for them, which at that time was equal to one week's salary in Australia. I explained that the little bags had cost me less that five shillings, but he insisted on the three pounds. So I asked for a pair of scissors, and, surprisingly, they gave them to me and watched as I cut up the two little bags and gave the pieces to the officer. He was astonished, but finally could not charge me.

The airplane was a real passenger plane -
not like the one from Bucharest to Bari. If I
recollect well, it was only an hour's flight.

At the airport I was greeted by our friends
and their little daughters. I was sorry to tell
them what had happened to their gifts, but they
didn't mind and they took me home.

For a few days we went around Sydney,
seeing the sights and finding the best
employment office for me to get a job. The best
was the government employment office because it
was free. I went and met a very nice woman who
interviewed me. I got a job outside Sydney in a
small hotel, which was mainly for well-to-do old
people. The salary was good, and the prospect
of working in a hotel again was great. I still
had a wonderful letter from Mr. Marentchich
from the Budapest Ritz, which, of course, by
that time did not exist. It had been bombed
away. This job also gave me a room as well as
board. I celebrated with our friends, happy
that I wouldn't be a burden to them.

The following week the Wangaratta arrived
and the captain brought my luggage. We had a
very pleasant lunch together. I had to promise
to keep in touch with him, and he said he would
see me every time he called in at the port. He
also took my parent's address and, as he
promised me, he called them and told them about
our voyage. He was a great old man.

The day after I moved to the hotel. I
couldn't have asked for a better job...or so I
thought. A middle aged Australian couple owned
the hotel, a young English woman and and
Australian boy were the reception crew. In a
couple of days I got to know the people of the
hotel by name. I noticed that when they came
downstairs and went to the girl to ask for a
stamp, she would bark at them and say she was
too busy. So I piped up and asked if I could
help and gladly gave them what they wished.

This went on until the end of the week, and
I noticed that the owner seemed to like my
manners, but his wife did not! She called me in
on Monday and told me that I must pack and leave
immediately.

I was stunned. I asked her if I had done
anything wrong. She said no, and offered to pay
me another week's salary if I would just leave
as soon as possible.

I was devastated. I couldn't understand
why I was fired for the first time in my life.
I called our friends and asked if I could sleep
at their place until I could find a new job.
The next day I went back to the employment
office. The woman just laughed off the whole
episode. I asked her why she was laughing as I
considered this a very serious matter. She then
told me that the reason I was fired was that
they were afraid that in no time I would take
over the hotel. All the people were asking who

the new pleasant girl was who smiled and didn't push them around. The agency lady explained that I had no intention or money to take over her business, but she insisted that she knew foreigners and that I would take over.

What a crazy woman! Lckily, I found a job as a receptionist in the old, but at that time still good Metropole Hotel in the center of the city. I also found a room which was not in a very good district, but I needed a place to live. The job was good, but there was not much to do in Sydney in 1948 and 49. I could go to some concerts in an unheated concert hall where the artists had to warm their hands before they played, or I could go to the cinema where I could see the same movie over and over again.

After nine o'clock at night, Sydney was dead. You couldn't even get a cup of coffee. I understand all that had changed now, and life is vital as it is in the States, and still growing. Somehow I had picked the wrong time. It was also not a good time for a woman alone, or for that matter, for a man. And as in Sweden, I did not get in touch with some rich friend of my family's for fear that he would think I was asking for help. I did, however, visit him two weeks before my departure to the States.

Around Easter time during the second year of my employment in the Metropole, two brothers from Rumania who were living in the hotel for a while asked me if I wanted to work for them as a

125

manager. They had just bought a small hotel and
needed someone with experience. I told them I
would think it over. They came after me every
day, and I had a dream that this job would give
me more money. I would be able to bring my
parents out. They promised everything. Stupid
me. I listened, and just before Easter, I left
the good Metropole Hotel.

You can imagine my disappointment after
they showed me to a small room which was
supposed to be my living quarters. It had
nothing in it but a bed. They had promised me a
flat in the hotel. They then took me to the
kitchen where there were dishes piled up to the
ceiling. As an excuse, they said that the
dishwasher had just quit and asked if I would
please wash everything, and then wash the
windows and baby-sit for their two year old son
as the nanny had just quit.

I was so astonished that it took me some
time to answer that there was no way that I
would do these things. I came as a manager and
not as dishwasher, window cleaner or baby
sitter. One of them screamed at me that the
Australians would do it. Only a bloody European
would not! I told him to get an Australian. I
would not work.

He did at least let me stay in that
wretched room for the night. In the morning I
found a nice room in the suburbs through an ad
in the paper. It was owned by a European

126

family. I settled in and went directly back to get my old job in the Metropole.

Mr. Fox, the manager, was very nice, but he told me that he had already hired a girl. She seemed to be very good and he couldn't fire her. After all, I had left them at the busiest time of the year just before Easter.

Oh what I would have given to be back in Sweden just then, feeling the love of my friends, having my job back at the Bank, and walking the streets of Stockholm.

I had chosen this miserable existence and now I was the only one who could do anything about it. It wasn't easy. Finally I found a Chinese restaurant where I was hired as a hostess but, in reality, I was a "bouncer." Really! I was the one who had to get rid of guests who became drunk and misbehaved. My boss was from the north of China. He was very tall and very well dressed and very, very arrogant. He was a bachelor in love with his very beautiful sister-in-law, to whom he made love right in the telephone booth of the restaurant.

A couple of nights after I started this job I was just about to throw out a very tall noisy drunk when a man walked in. He was the young pianist, Thomas, with whom I had organized concerts in Aradin. The man with him was an English impresario. It was a great shock and surprise. Of all the places in the world we

127

might meet, it would be in Sydney, Australia and in a Chinese restaurant! Thomas was already married. He and his wife were in Australia temporarily until they could get to America where his wife had relatives. The Englishman was worried that I would take over, but I assured him that I could not be an impresario because it was not my field and I did not have my good connection Marika any more, not in Australia.

It was an interesting evening, and there were many more of them. During this time I looked for a more suitable job. I finally found one in a very good chain restaurant call Cahills. There, at least I was a hostess, although also a part-time waitress.

In general, the job was uninteresting but at least it fed me and paid for my room. My mood was very low. It seemed that anything I did in Australia turned out the wrong way. I wrote some children's stories which I was sure would be a favorite with kids, but not so in Australia at that time. All I received was my manuscript back and a polite form letter with a suggestion that I write cowboy stories, which is what children were really interested in. I was down in the dumps for the first time in my life. Somehow, I couldn't see change coming.

I must say I did meet some very interesting and delightful people in Cahills. Among them were a Doctor Couple and a few nice women in fairly high positions. One lady finally asked me if I would like to join the Soroptimist International Club.

I had to confess that I had never heard of it. She explained the origin of the club. Actually a Rotary member who had organized this professional women's organization. The name was derived from the Latin "Soro" for woman,"optimo" for best, hence, "best for women." It was an honor to be invited to their meetings. I was a hostess of a well known restaurant and they didn't have any members in this category yet. I was asked if I would care to join. I, of course, did so. Ever since 1949, I have been a member and I am now a life member and still very much interested in the organization.

Still, life was not happy for me. Even the news from Sweden was not good. My father had done a foolish thing. He was not happy with his new job within the government. The money was not enough, so he changed to a Hungarian job and was immediately told to leave the country as the office belonged to the Hungarian Government. I wrote to the police chief of Stockholm, who I knew, and explained that he was my father. I was sure he had only taken the job because he needed more money, not because he wished to work for the Hungarian government. It was an endless few weeks and I felt helpless being so far away. I was hoping that perhaps they would remember me and it would help. Finally, I got the word that it had worked out and my parents would be

1948, working Hotel Metropole, Sydney.

On the way to the U.S. 1951.

allowed to remain in Sweden.

With that over, and even with my job fairly secure and with my new Club and new friends, I found myself still extremely lonely. For the first time I was really unhappy. Somehow there seemed no future and I was truly sorry to have left my beloved Sweden. I didn't have any money to return.

Then, when I was at the lowest point of my life, a miracle happened again. A letter arrived from the American Embassy informing me that my visa had been granted and by the 15th of June, 1951, I had to be in the United States.

This posed a problem. There were no airplanes flying regularly to the United States from Australia, nor were there any boats. I had to find some kind of transportation. After many inquiries, I found a cargo boat, an American ship. They had one place, which I immediately reserved. Now I had to find the money to pay for my passage as I had not one cent to my name.

Through my parents and my dearest Aunt Rosa and other family members in America, two days before departure I finally had the money together. I hadn't any money for any extras on the trip, which I discovered would take seven weeks.

As fate would have it, once again I was lucky. One of the members of the Soroptimist club wanted to come to the States. At that time you were required to have at least $500.00 dollars in an American bank as security that you would not remain after the allotted time of your visit. I told her that I would carry this money with me and deposit it in a certain bank in New York. She agreed. Therefore, besides one lucky penny I had had for a long time, it was her money that gave me at least some security on the long voyage. I did spend twenty dollars out of this amount.

Fortunately when I arrived in New York, some very dear friends took the remainder and deposited the entire $500.00 in a bank saying that the twenty dollars was a gift instead of flowers. So my friend and I were happy and all turned out well.

The day I left was again memorable, as all my leave-takings had been. I had not been happy in Sydney but I had made some good friends and saying good-by is never easy. This ship was not the Swedish boat Wangaratta. We had only twelve passengers, and I shared a cabin with an elderly lady. We only had a shower and there was no lounge or living room. The dining room was the center of everything. The captain was not my wonderful old Captain either, but a highly unpleasant man whose cargo was far more important than his passengers. The food was all frozen and cockroaches walked on our table. The only civilized place to stay was on deck in the blazing sun.

There were other benefits, however. I was on my way. The weather could not have been nicer as we sailed from Sydney. Once again the emotions played hard with my mind. Once more I had a new life when the one I had just left had been such a disappointment. I had also left behind new experiences, new learning, new joy and new sorrows. I was somewhat less than enthused about my future in a new land where I would once again have to work hard to succeed.

The only consolation on this trip to America was the anticipated joy of having Aunt Rosa, Lydia--now married--and Anita, Zoltan and their daughter and newborn son to meet me upon my arrival.

I sat quietly for a time, just to think it over, and try to understand what was happening to me. How would I repay the loans for the trip to my family and friends? I looked around to find some face that I would enjoy on this cargo boat. I knew we were twelve passengers, but I can only remember a few of them.

I remember my roommate. The elderly lady lived in Sydney for a few years and was now on the way to live with her daughter in America. She was a nice lady and we got along very well together. Later, in America, I visited her and her family.

I remember a couple engaged to be married. He was Australian and she was a Canadian. He was very thin with an irritable nature and a rather violent temper. I am not a card player but, as we had nothing to do on this ship, we played simple rummy. When, by chance, I won, he would throw the cards in my face. His fiance was also very thin, spoke seldom, and was very reserved. She seemed to be afraid of something. They were ill matched, and I remember hoping that somehow they would have a happy life in Canada.

The only other passenger I remember was an alcoholic American, to whom I never spoke other than saying good morning and good evening. Despite this, I learned through one of the officers that he wished me to know that he wanted to marry me. He told them to inform me that he was rich, had a new Pontiac large enough for a bedroom as the seats would fold out into a bed. Any young immigrant girl should be happy to marry a man possessing a car like this, which indicated his prosperity.

I answered back by way of an officer that I didn't wish to get married for a long while. I said, that although I was probably a foolish girl to ignore his offer, and perhaps wouldn'' again get such a wonderful opportunity, I simply could not marry him.

This second-hand shipboard romance continued through intermediaries for a time until I was told he would commit suicide if I wouldn't marry him. Fortunately, the ship's

officers talked him out of this foolish nonsense
and as far as I know, there was no death on the
ship. As a matter of fact, our strange romance
was the only entertainment on the boat!

From Sydney we went to Brisbane and then
turned back to the Tasman Sea. We did not stop
until we arrived in Trinadad. There we spent
three days. It was raining and the crew could
not work on the cargo they had to pick up.

It was a benefit for us. Here at least we
could get off the ship and walk in the city. It
was so oil rich that in some parts of the city
the oil was coming right out of the earth. It
was fascinating for me to see the ladies
carrying heavy loads on their heads and to enjoy
the colorful dresses they wore. It seemed to be
such a bustling, colorful world. It was very
warm.

One night we all slept in a very beautiful
hotel with a swimming pool fed by fresh water
from a wonderful waterfall that came down the
mountainside behind the hotel. It was fantastic
to swim in it at midnight with moonlight shining
on the wonderland.

I also had an escort, not the gentleman
from the ship who wished to marry me but a big,
live monkey that took a fancy to me while we
were dancing in a garden adjoining the dining
room. These monkeys were all over the place and
this particular monkey jumped right on my

shoulder and wouldn't let anyone dance with me. He was holding me tight and said something in monkey language which I couldn't understand. After the dancing I was quite sure that he would not follow me to the pool. I wasn't in the water a moment, however, when this very excited monkey jumped all around, ordering me out of the water to follow him.

It took the management about an hour to calm him down and make him understand that I had to sleep somewhere where he could not follow me. Some romance!

In any case, it was a welcome change to be off that dirty ship and eat something other than frozen food while watching cockroaches eat from our table.

Then we came to the Panama Canal and we saw a Swedish vessel with a marvelous canvas pool. We asked our captain for the same but of course he refused.

The Canal was another great adventure. It is an incredible experience to go through those docks with the water going down and then up and then down again. It was fascinating. And the weather was incredibly hot. We got off in Panama City for a few hours, just time enough to get some cool drinks and ice cream. Panama City was depressing in 1951. It seemed very poor, and rather like something left over from older times. We were even happy to get back on our ship.

Finally, we were on our way to Boston on the
final leg of our adventure. One morning as I
sat on deck in the blazing sun, I saw an island
in the distance. There were palm trees and
monkeys. I was so surprised, as we were far out
at sea, so I ran to one of the officers and
pulled him to the spot where I had been sitting
and showed him the island in the distance. He
looked at me as though I were crazy, and told me
that there was no island. He said this happened
to many people. It was an illusion.

Well, if it was an illusion, it was a
lovely way of breaking up a very boring trip.
There was no Captain here with a big library, or
any place to sit and read quietly. The
entertainment consisted of giving nicer names to
different passengers. The officers wouldn't
tell me what name they had given me. They felt
that as I was not an American, perhaps I would
take offense. Finally, after lots of cajoling,
they told me my name was "Sweater Girl," and
explained that this wasn't a bad name, but very
flattering. Jane Russell, look out!

On June the 10th, we were nearing the
harbor of Boston. That was the time to smell
"Boston Beans." What an arrival this was! I
didn't feel like an immigrant, but like a queen
who had just come back to her country. As we
sailed into port, the ship was very tall in the
water and the people looked very small on shore.

136

Then I heard a voice from the pier. A woman's voice called, "Agnes, is that you?"

I answered that indeed it was. She explained that she was the president of the Soroptimist Club. Then I saw Anita's cousin, an old friend of mine from Switzerland, who was awaiting my arrival. It was really exciting. I hadn't expected anyone to pick me up and as I looked down, there seemed to be a great crowd!

It turned out that the President of the Sydney Soroptimist Club had notified the Boston club that I was coming on the cargo boat. For seven weeks they had followed the route we were taking. When I got off the ship there were three ladies the President, a member of the Boston club, and a member of the English club, who was leaving the next morning.

All this made me more excited about my arrival. I flew right into the arms of my new friends and my relatives. My Soroptimist friends asked if I could come that afternoon for cocktails so that they could celebrate the English woman's departure and my arrival together.

Going through customs was an amazing experience as well. Everyone gave me a lovely smile of welcome to the country. They just marked my bags and out I went. Now I really thought that perhaps I was dreaming. This couldn't be happening to me, but it was. I went first to my friends' home, showered, and changed. Then they took me to the Soroptimist Club.

There were more surprises. First off, I had never before drunk a cocktail and also, coming from that boat, I didn't think that such good food still existed! There were lobster and shrimp and other wonderful foods. What a pleasure it was. To top it off I had never seen television. As it was Sunday, the Ed Sullivan Show was on. Through the years I continued to watch this show, with many happy recollections, until Ed Sullivan's death. This was the glorious beginning of my new life in America.

CHAPTER 7

Well, there I was, in the United States, with dreams of a new life, better than I had had for the past three years at least. Yes, all my dreams have come true here. For thirty-five years I have had a wonderful life, and now my involvement once again with the Raoul Wallenberg case. But first, my arrival.

That first night in Boston, June 10, 1951, I went to my initiation in my Club. They also promised to look for a job for me at once so that I could remain in Boston. My friend and his wife sat for hours with me, talking about all that had occurred between 1939 and 1951.

We called Aunt Rosa and Lydia and of course Anita and Zoltan. I told them that I might possibly stay in Boston. At that point their four-year-old daughter came to the phone and declared in a very annoyed voice, that she had especially brushed her teeth for me and complained that now I wasn't coming to New York. As I couldn't disappoint a child, particularly my best friends' little daughter, I immediately gave up the idea of staying in Boston. I told her that I would take a train to New York in the morning so that on Monday afternoon she could show me her beautiful white teeth. That calmed her down and I believe it also made my friends very happy.

In the morning I called the president of

the Soroptimist Club, and informed her of my decision. She agreed that I couldn't disappoint a child and laughingly we said our good-byes. I again thanked her.

With great anticipation, I left on the train and arrived in New York. I was met by Lydia and her new husband. There are not words to describe our meeting. We drove to Anita's place and there again, it was just too emotional for words. It was as though we had never separated. I immediately went to the bedroom to see the 6-month-old son. He woke up for just a moment, long enough to give me a most welcome smile, and then went peacefully back to sleep.

What a great feeling it was! No more loneliness, or searching for new friends. I had it all! I was here in the tiny apartment with them.

Anita did not like the color of my hair, which was bleached out from the constant strong sun on the cargo boat. We went off to a hairdresser so that I could look as stylish as an American Sweater Girl, which in a short time I managed to do.

During my first week, Anita's friend hired me as a mother's helper on Fire Island for the following week. In the days between the two Sundays, we had so much to catch up on, not having seen each other since 1945. I also had so much enjoyment playing with the children that the time went quickly.

On the following Sunday, my cousin Eleanor and her husband Bob, came to visit Anita.

There I was, newly arrived and without a job. And yet I refused Bob's great offer. They were owners of a big spice factory and Bob offered me a job as an assistant to the bookkeeper at a weekly salary of $50.00 which I think was a good salary in 1951.

You can perhaps imagine the look on cousin Bob's face when I said no thank you. Everyone looked at me as though I was out of my mind. Poor Bob had to question my decision, so I told him that I knew nothing of bookkeeping, and although I was sure I could learn it quickly, I didn't feel I should work for my own family. I explained that if he was not satisfied with me, he couldn't comfortably fire me, and that if I didn't like the job I wouldn't be able to tell him.

I asked him to allow me to come and apply for the job if I couldn't find another suitable position. Although they all thought I was crazy, they also understood what I meant. It was a lovely gesture on Bob's part to offer the job.

When Monday arrived, I went to Fire Island. The children were sweet and the grownups pleasant. However, Fire Island disturbed me

141

somewhat. I had never seen men kissing or
making love to each other. Altogether, I had
little knowledge of sex. I therefore found it
difficult to understand why parents with little
boys would choose to buy a house in the
environment.

But each to his own taste. That week also
passed and I was paid twenty-five dollars. I
felt so rich!

In 1951, twenty-five dollars went a long
way - so far in fact that I ordered the National
Geographic magazine, bought a season ticket to
the Philadelphia Orchestra, and went for my
"first papers," which at that time were still
required from immigrants who wanted to become
U.S. citizens. The lady at the immigration
office told me that in her twenty years, I was
the first to apply after only two weeks in the
country.

Oh, I was happy that I had finally come
home! I had nowhere else I had to go. Finally
I could stop being a child of the winds. Here I
would find my happiness and tranquillity for
which I had so long searched.

Now I had two countries of origin as I saw
it. One will forever be Sweden, my paradise,
where I felt the first real freedom of my life.
And now the United States.

In my first chosen country, Sweden, it was

not just the new found freedom, but the great memory of my mission with Raoul, the man who had changed me from a shy person into a real personality, someone who cared. Also in Sweden I felt very much "wanted." When a person made fun of my accent I was happy, because if the person had not corrected me, he would not have cared. I was part of their daily life, good and bad. It was a great lesson for me to teach them English. It had been great being in their Christmas play.

In America, although I had just arrived, the feeling was much the same. I would be free and I would not be a second class citizen. I belonged here.

So in the third week of my sojourn I answered an ad in the New York Times for a hostess job in Stouffers, a choice restaurant. At that time there was one opposite Grand Central Station. On the way to my interview I ventured for the first time to take the subway. In 1951 the subway was a great pleasure. I don't know what has happened since then. At that time there was no graffiti. It was clean and pleasant, and on time. Today? Well, please forget it.

In any event, that morning I stood on the platform, trying to find out exactly which way I should go to Manhattan. A lady came up to me and asked if I was a Soroptimist, as I was wearing the emblem. Naturally we became friends and she traveled with me to New York, inviting me for Wednesday's meeting. She showed me where the employment office for Stouffers was on Fifth Avenue.

Needless to say, I got the job immediately. The pay was not much, but it provided me all my meals, and on the weekends Stouffers gave all their breads, pastries and other baked goods to their employees, which was wonderful for me. I could supply my darling family with all these things.

I worked from about eleven in the morning to about two-thirty p.m., and then again from five to about eight p.m. It gave me a break to go to the movies on 3rd Avenue which at that time showed great French and Italian movie like "La Strada." It also gave me time to write a ballet for a little four-foot waitress who was a dancer. I was fascinated by her and I hope that one day this ballet can be performed.

I was also looking for an apartment or room, so that I would not disturb Zoltan and Anita. I finally found a room at 96th and Riverside. It was pleasant, but I was hoping it would not be forever. My weekends were, of course, spent with the children so that Anita and Zoltan could go out. I enjoyed being there anyway as I liked Queens more than Manhattan and was happy to go there every weekend.

While I worked at Stouffers, I met many

nice people who came there from the banks and the airline offices surrounding the restaurant. I befriended some of them and we got talking. I told them that it must be fun to work for an airline and mentioned that I spoke several languages. I was hoping that perhaps I would have an opportunity to work for one also.

One dear couple who ran the newspaper concession in the airline terminal promised to look into it. My friends again told me that it would be impossible to get a job at any airline as they would not employ foreigners. But, as you can already see, I have a hard head and just as Raoul Wallenberg never gave up, I too felt that nothing was impossible.

While I was waiting for this possibility, my boss tried to get me a raise in salary of about fifty cents an hour. My new friends got me some papers to fill out for a job at Pan American Airlines and even a portable typewriter. They helped me to fill out the application properly and I went the next afternoon for an interview.

The gentleman I spoke with was very kind, but he explained that Pan Am paid very little and suggested that I try TWA. I told him that I didn't know anyone over there so he picked up the telephone and called someone. Then he told me to go next door and pick up the application forms.

I thought it was nice of him to help me and of course I did as he suggested.

At TWA they were very helpful, telling me that I could go to Kennedy Airport (it was then still Idlewild) at nine a.m. for an interview, since I had to go to work at eleven. The woman even made an appointment for me for Thursday morning.

In the meantime my boss in Stouffers, an Englishman, got me my raise! I went to the airport and had my interview in German with a nice young lady. She made an appointment for me with the manager of reservations for Friday morning.

I was really excited. I went the next morning with mixed feelings. I really believed that I could not get the job. Well, again I was interviewed by a very nice gentleman. He talked to me for quite a long time and then decided that I would be good at the ticket counter. He sent me right over there. I was given the job immediately and I was asked to start the following Monday.

Now I had a great dilemma. My boss had just gotten me a raise at Stouffers. I explained this to the gentleman who had hired me. I asked him to let me talk to my boss at Stouffers as I felt I was betraying him. After all, he had tried to help me.

He was surprised at my loyalty and said that I should call him immediately after I had spoken to my boss. Better yet, I should come back to him right after I had spoken with him.

It was still before eleven, so I went to the boss, and I lied. I told him that my doctor felt that it was too much for me to stand on my feet and that I had to quit. I also thanked him for all his help.

He looked at me and said, "Agnes, you got a better job, I bet. I'm happy for you. And for your information, I am leaving Stouffers too. Please tell me where your new job is and I'll give you a reference." I was surprised and very happy. I told him where I was going, and then went off to TWA. When I got to the office of my new boss he told me that he had heard many recommendations, but never one as good as my former boss at Stouffers had given me. He asked me again to start on Monday at the TWA ticket counter. The salary was more than double that at Stouffers and I would also get schooling while I was being paid.

What a celebration that was! Anita and cousin Bob couldn't believe it. I had twelve very happy years with Trans World.

That last day at Stouffers went quickly. I had to thank all of my new friends for their help in this matter, and my boss for giving me such a fine recommendation. So this was my last

147

weekend with my dear family. On Monday I started at the 42nd Street office to learn about ticketing and the handling of passengers. From the first moment it was a fascinating job. My supervisor and colleagues were wonderful. All in all, another dream had come through. I was making good money, and had marvelous travel possibilities.

I had hardly worked there a week when, by chance, I got a bachelor apartment in Forest Hills, within walking distance of Anita's apartment. The rent was something like thirty-five dollars a month. It was a nice sized room with a kitchenette, bathroom and little entrance. It was just enough and it was private. Later on I got a new refrigerator and the rent went up to forty-two dollars. I understand that in this day and age, whoever lives in that apartment now pays over two hundred dollars a month for it.

At the end of my three weeks of training I was transferred to the office in the Waldorf Astoria Hotel. In a few months that office was closed and I went to the middle of the world at the Rockefeller Center office.

While I worked at the Waldorf, I celebrated my six months anniversary with TWA. I boldly asked my boss if I could get a free ticket to Europe as I wished to visit my parents, especially for my father's birthday on January 21st. As we did not fly to Stockholm, he

148

promised to see what he could do on KLM or Scandinavian Airlines. Getting days off was easy. Among ourselves we could exchange, so I could easily get two weeks off. The thought of not only seeing my parents, but also seeing my beloved Stockholm was highly exciting. My dear boss, Marty, had the sales person from KLM visit me in the office to get some information from me.

Then, the next week, Marty told me that he wanted to take me out for my official coffee break with the KLM salesman as, unfortunately, I could not get a free ticket.

I was disappointed, of course, but went with them for coffee. As we sipped coffee and talked about the possibility of another time, the salesman handed me an envelope. Very surprised, I opened it and guess what? There was my official pass to Sweden from KLM. Of course I burst into tears. So much kindness in such a short time was overwhelming. Again I was ashamed to be such a lucky girl, surviving the war the way I had and now having all this happiness.

The day I left, the office gave me a beautiful corsage to pin on my suit, and asked the hostess to give me a free drink on the airplane. I left the Waldorf in a dream. I couldn't believe this was happening to me!

We flew to Amsterdam. There the weather

was not very good. Some flights had to be canceled. I was downhearted as I wanted to be in Stockholm for my father's birthday. As I walked around, evidently disturbed, a Scandinavian Airline Passenger Relations man came to me and asked if he could help. I told him that I was a TWA employee and that I was stuck. He said that there was one Scandinavian flight leaving and the he could get me on it since there was an agreement between the airlines to help each other.

So, of course, I got on the flight and was there for the birthday.

I had a fantastic time in my beloved country, seeing my parents and all my dear friends. Time passed too quickly, on the way back I flew via London, where my aunt and cousin who had just married lived. At that time there was still a shortage of food in Britain, so mother packed meat and other goodies for them. It was wonderful to see these relatives too, and then I was off again, back to the States.

In the meantime our new building, the East Side Terminal, opened or was in the process of opening, and I was transferred back to Rockefeller Center. It was wonderful there. Then I went back to the 42nd Street office but very shortly I was down in the new office of the East Side Terminal.

We did everything there, from ticketing to

handling baggage. I was there almost ten full
years. It was exhausting at times, but always
interesting. I worked all the weekends and
opened the office every morning at seven a.m.
This schedule gave me time to travel all over
the country on the weekdays, and although I had
not time for much social life, at least I got to
concerts which was my greatest pleasure.

In 1956 I became an American citizen and
got my first American passport. At last I
didn't have to travel with a "nansen passport."
Very proudly, I took my first trip as an
American. I went to Spain and Italy. I visited
Rome, of course, and then went to Portofino. It
was very early in the morning when I arrived and
only milk carriages were visible. I got a horse
and carriage and in this calm, beautiful morning
I was driven to the hotel.

It was like a fairy land--just the milk
man, a few newspaper boys but otherwise just
calm beauty! The hotel overlooked the sea and
the tiny city of Portofino. Mr. Nodvornik, the
manager of the hotel was very kind to me. The
manager from Madrid had written to him about me
so he was like a long lost friend.

Of course in Madrid I spoke about Raoul
Wallenberg and his great accomplishments to the
manager. He was so interested that he had me
give an interview to the daily paper, with
pictures and all. However, for the newspaper I
could not talk about the mission in Budapest as

151

it was still the era of Franco. So I had to talk about the woman's role in America and what Soroptimist meant. I was thoroughly briefed by my friend as to what I should and should not say.

At least here in Portofino there was no talk of war or of the past. It was all geared toward the future and the wonderful fishing village. This seemed right to me then. I felt I was at the end of the world. There was nowhere to go except backwards or to stay here in this lovely spot.

Mr. Nodvornik was also very helpful in finding my old boyfriend and his family for me. They were not too far away in Genova. How happy I was to have this information. I called them on the phone at once. It was a wonderful surprise. I was alive and they were alive. I took a bus to Genova and there was Nenen, his wife, his two sons, and daughter. I stayed only one day there and then left by train for Rome. He said I was like a meteor that had flown down from heaven and then disappeared again. It was a lovely meeting. Past loves can be very welcoming and heartwarming.

By that time my parents left Sweden for Argentina, where they expected to find the promised land. They were doing very well. They had a small pension in Mar Del Plata, a seashore town with casinos and a good life. But now that I was a citizen, they wanted to come to America.

I tried to tell them that life without money for elderly people was not too easy but they wanted to come anyway.

So in 1957, they arrived in America, traveling free courtesy of Pan American. Next door to my one room apartment I found an apartment for them, furnished it and had it ready by the time they arrived, although I was broke! At least I had my job, which I loved.

Mother started to do catering and papa helped her. They established quite a good little business. I bought season tickets to the Philadelphia Orchestra and we sat up high. The acoustics were excellent and the tickets cheap. The old lady who also sat in our row was by now a friend. She was happy to meet my parents. So life went on with work and concerts and not much else, but it was happy.

In the season of 1959-1960, papa asked me not to buy him tickets to the concerts any more as the steps were too much for him and he didn't enjoy the music as much as mother and I did. That season I only bought two for us. At the first concert we wondered who would be sitting next to us. There was an oriental gentleman sitting in papa's seat. He wore a crew cut and a very dark suit. He looked extremely intelligent and obviously liked the same music we did. Of course our lady friend was still there.

By that time in 1959, I was very set in my ways with work, travel, and music. One thing I did not want to hear about was marriage. I had too good a job, could go and do as I pleased, had lots of friends and I could not imagine being married.

Life went on as usual and around November the old lady beside us finally couldn't stand it any more. She had to know who the young oriental gentleman was who enjoyed the same music. Very politely she asked him if he was Chinese? Very politely he replied that no, he was Japanese.

I really don't know why I was curious myself but I listened carefully to the conversation. So he was Japanese and liked music.

The next month came and our friend was again curious about him. She asked, "Young man, what are you doing in this country?" Our dear man again very politely answered this extremely rude question. He said that he was a medical doctor. Now I knew a lot about him but of course he knew nothing about us, except that mother and I always arrived early. He was there even earlier and as we mounted the steps, he would already be there and get up politely to let us in and say "Good evening." That was all he did all those months.

Finally February rolled around. It was the

coldest, snowiest day and mother and I both had
bad colds. I had a fever and a swollen tongue
but we didn't want to lose our money so I
decided to come to town and sell the tickets.
As I stood there in the cold entrance-way of
Carnegie Hall I decided that the Japanese doctor
might be disappointed if we didn't come. I made
up my mind to sell only one ticket. This I did
very quickly and I called home to tell my mother
that as I came all that way in the cold, I would
stay for the concert after all.

I went up, but suddenly I felt so feverish
it was really difficult to make those steps. My
oriental friend noticed and got up from his seat
and walked down to meet me. The place was very
empty that night as many people had stayed away
because of the weather.

As he came down all he said was "You sick?"
I answered, "Yes," and sat down. At
intermission he asked me if I would have a cup
of tea with him after the performance? I said I
would.

So after the concert we went down behind
Carnegie Hall on 56th Street to a wonderful
coffee shop which isn't there anymore. It was
called the Peacock Alley. We sat down to have a
cup of tea and lots of talk. It was near
midnight when we finished, and, miraculously, my
fever had disappeared. I felt great.

My new friend galantly went all the way on

155

the subway to Forest Hills with me and then had to go all the way back to upper Manhattan to the Womens' Hospital.

Our great romance started by listening during early evenings through two telephones on two radios to Pablo Casals Master classes. We had one date to see a Peter Sellers movie, "The Mouse that Roared," and the telephone dates continued.

I called Lydia to tell her that I was dating a Japanese doctor. She was interested. She had lived for a couple of years with her husband in Tokyo and she wanted to meet him. Unfortunately we had no time to see her as our schedule had not changed and we were both too busy.

In the middle of March we went to see "Can-Can" and after then we went for supper on 42nd Street to the Brass Rail. Over two corned beef sandwiches, my dear Masa asked me if I would marry him! Now, here was a girl who didn't ever want to get married, knew little about this man, and didn't even know if he would be staying in the United States or not. My heart answered and I said, "Yes". I never felt such inner peace. It was quite strange. I felt that I never wanted anyone else but him and this was what I had wanted all my life. I knew that we liked the same music but I also felt that many other things would also be common loves for both of us.

I wakened my parents at six in the morning to tell them and also called Lydia. We became engaged just before our March concert at Carnegie Hall and as we sat down, my husband-to-be turned to the old lady and told her that we were engaged. She was so stunned that she didn't understand what he had said. He repeated it and explained that it was because of her that we were engaged. Then she understood and there was great happiness for all of us.

Everyone in my office was shocked because as far as they knew I didn't even date. The office gave us a wonderful "bridal shower." We started preparations for my wedding at once and faced the question. Where and how? We both had many friends already but we couldn't possibly invite everyone. Masa only earned sixty dollars a month at that time and I about five hundred. I had some debts too.

Nevertheless I got my passes for "free travel" for two for a three week honeymoon to Europe. This was a great surprise for my future husband, and a very exciting one. He had never been to Europe before and was anxious to see it. We wanted to go to Paris first and from there to Switzerland to see my family and then on to Sweden to see my friends.

We actually had two weddings. One was the official wedding on the 27th of April before a justice of the peace in Queens, with my father

157

and my cousin Ferko as witnesses. Afterwards we had a great dinner at my parents' home. Then I asked my cousin to please take Masa home to the Bronx, where he then worked at Lebanon Hospital. Ferko looked at me in bewilderment and called me to the kitchen to ask me if I was crazy. Why was I sending my husband home? I had to explain that my office officially only gave me leave from Friday. This was only Wednesday, and I had to get up at four in the morning and Masa had to work early too. There was no other way so he took him home, shaking his head.

Of course Masa called Japan and told his family about his forthcoming marriage. Everybody was surprised and happy for us at the same time. I am sure that for a moment it must have been a shock for the family to know that he was not marrying a Japanese girl, but they knew Masa and were sure that his judgment must be right. What a great family they have turned out to be, my family in Japan. I am a very lucky girl!

Our second wedding, or rather reception, was at noon on Saturday, April 30th, in a beautiful baroque building belonging to the Japanese Embassy. Masa had a friend there who was "head chef" and he organized the reception for about 150 people. There were all kinds of fantastic foods: shrimp, lobster, and almost anything one might wish. That, together with the champagne and Bach in the background, made it perfect. We had such a good time that again cousin Ferko had to remind us that we should get out of there. We had a chauffeured limousine (courtesy of cousin Ferko) to take us home for our baggage and on to the airport where we spent the night in the International Hotel, this time courtesy of TWA.

The next day was May Day, pouring rain. We invited my parents to have lunch with us at the airport and then our flight was canceled because of weather conditions. One flight however, did leave and my friends at the airport took some full-paying passengers off to let the honeymooners go. Everyone was so wonderful.

Our trip, of course, was very exciting. Paris was all we had hoped for and meeting the family and friends in Switzerland and Sweden was the greatest. What a honeymoon! One thing might have spoiled it, but it didn't. I finally found, in my beloved husband, someone who believed my story of Raoul Wallenberg. During the entire three weeks we talked about Raoul and my big-hearted husband cried quite a lot to hear of the treatment Raoul had received for all his selfless help to mankind. It was a great relief to finally share this with someone who really understood and lovingly tried to help. Sharing it with another human being was so important.

The family in Zurich was great. My Hungarian aunt was married to a Russian, my first cousin married a Swede, the second a Swiss, the third a· Frenchman and now us. A

league of nations. It was a wonderful meeting.
In Sweden we had the same reception and
happiness. I enjoyed showing Stockholm to my
new husband with great pride. One night we went
to the Opera House all dressed in evening gown
and dinner jacket, only to find everyone else in
sweaters and slacks. It was somewhat
uncomfortable, but made us laugh in our misery
for it really was funny.

On our arrival back in the U.S. we found
that we had the good fortune to have gotten a
four room apartment in the next house. That's
where our super lived and he wanted a doctor in
the house. So with great ceremony we left my
little bachelor apartment and moved to our new
two bedroom apartment. The noise was hard to
get used to, as the apartment overlooked the
railway, but we got used to it quickly. On our
first anniversary, my husband invited my parents
to a very great home-made Japanese dinner. It
worked just perfectly. We had a good time.

The second time we did this, it didn't turn
out quite as well, but at least we again had
great laughs. It was my husband's former boss
and his second wife who came. It was a very
snowy, winter day and Masa pulled out the shrimp
to defrost them when the phone rang. We were
told that the airplane had been delayed and they
were going to be an hour late.

Instead of leaving the shrimp out, my dear
one put it back in the freezer. In a while they

160

arrived, very cold. I immediately served them drinks and hors d'ouevres, while Masa started dinner. In a very happy mood we sat down for dinner. All went well until we bit into the marvelous fried shrimp. Unfortunately it was completely frozen inside. Our guests ate it with great pleasure, totally warmed by the good drinks Masa and I had to cover our embarrassment and our laughter. But what would life be if everything always went smoothly? I think it would be boring.

During this time we didn't see each other too much. I had to get up at four a.m. every morning to open the TWA office at seven and Masa came home very late at night when I was already asleep.

On our second anniversary, we went to Italy for vacation and on our return we had quite a few surprises. The first was that Masa had gotten a government grant to work in Neuropathology at New York University which suddenly gave us nine thousand dollars more a year. We had not recovered from this good news when we found out that I was pregnant. This of course was the news of the century. Our happiness was incredible. It was an easy pregnancy. I walked to work every morning from 53rd Street to 38th Street and I talked to my not yet born child all the time. I was sure that he heard me and also I was sure that it would be a boy.

On February 8th, 1963, Taro John was born. We were ecstatic. Three months after his birth I went back to work full time. My parents looked after him for a few days a week, I was off two days and Masa was free on the weekends. It really worked out very well as both of us still had to work.

I did promise that when Taro was one year old I would stop working. At that time I stopped full time work, but continued on a part-time basis on the weekends in our reservation office. I was there one Saturday when I got the phone call from my husband telling me that he had just gotten a job paying nineteen thousand dollars a year. I told him not to kid me while I was working but he said he wasn't fooling. He was to start working part time at this new job the following week and that would bring him an extra three hundred dollars a month. In January he would start his job full time.

You can imagine my excitement. Taro's first birthday was celebrated with our last free pass to Spain. We visited Madrid first where I had a dear friend, Alfonso Font Yllen, the General Manager of the Palace Hotel. He advised us to come to his hotel instead of the Ritz, as we had a one year old child and the Ritz had much royalty and old people. He was afraid that a youngster would disturb them. Actually we shouldn't have worried as Taro behaved beautifully, ate everything and was quiet all through lunch.

One day we were walking in the city and we passed by a chocolate store. In the window there was a box of chocolates and it came with the most wonderful elf, all dressed up in red. We went in and bought it, not because of the chocolate but because of the elf. Taro was sleeping in the carriage as we walked around. When he wakened, we handed him the elf. For one moment he had a funny expression on his lovely face. Then he started to laugh and hug this dear toy. He took the elfs hat off, which was of course filled with candies, and as he was "bold" we nicknamed him Boldi. Today Taro is 25 years old but Boldi is still with us reminding us of our Spanish days.

We will never forget our departure day from Madrid. As we came down with the porter and our luggage, we saw Alfonso in striped trousers and morning coat going after a very handsome tall gentleman. I overheard him calling the man "Your Excellency." But of course it didn't make much of an impression on me as I was busy with my baby.

As we came to the door, Alfonso turned to us with a smile and then turned back to the tall gentleman and said, "Your Excellency, may I introduce my dear friends to you, Dr. and Mrs. Adachi and their little boy, Taro, from America." His Excellency kissed my hand, kissed my Taro commenting on his beauty and shook hands with my husband. Then with a big smile he

descended the steps to his waiting limousine. I
asked Alfonso who he was.   Laughing heartily,
his answer was simple.   It was the former King
of Italy, King Umberto, living in exile in
Portugal. Years after, we visited Portugal with
both of our children, and went to visit King
Umberto's villa in Escarol. We signed the guest
book, saying that we remembered his kiss on the
steps of the Palace Hotel and wished he could
kiss our second child now.

In any case, after our great stay in
Madrid, we went to Torremalinos to a hotel
recommended by Alfonso. That was when Taro
really started to walk and talk. There were
steps going up from one of the halls to our
rooms. Masa was holding Taro's hand and they
walked up and then down. They did this perhaps
three times, when suddenly my one year old son
stamped angrily on the ground and in a strong
voice said "No." He wouldn't go up again with
his father. We had to carry him upstairs. In
that hall there was a breakfront filled with
family heirlooms.   One was especially
interesting for Taro. There was a black bull
with white horns. He stood there fascinated and
pointed at this bull saying only "uh, uh, uh."
We told the proprietor about it. They were very
fond of Taro and on our departure they gave him
this precious bull as a present. We were
touched to say the least. Taro now had two great
friends, Boldi and the bull.

It was wonderful traveling with our child

and later with our children. We made our greatest friends through the children and I am sure we will all remember each one of those trips.

Every time I recall all these good times, I also remember my good fortune at being on my mission with Raoul Wallenberg and therefore having this wonderful time today in America. Without him, I and so many others would not be alive, much less enjoy all our good fortune. Why could not Raoul have been compensated for all the good he had done for humanity? No matter what our good fortune and where we traveled, I always thought of him.

So life went on. My husband's salary grew. I was pregnant again. We bought a house. The new baby was born in October, 1965. We moved when I was four months pregnant. As we didn't have enough money for a mover for all our things, we did it alone. I was carrying many things up three flights and thank God, as my dear husband is fond of telling me, I am as strong as a horse.

Shortly after Jiro's birth, my father got very ill and three months after our new son was born my father died. We were happy that at least he had know both of his grandsons. For quite a long time, little Taro wanted to go after his granddad. It was so hard to explain that granddad was now happy and we told him that he should be happy that he had that great memory of his grandfather as a playmate. It took a long time for the little one to realize that he would not be coming back.

My second baby was an unusual character. The second best in the world, after his brother. It is not the right word to say "second best" as both of our lovely children are the best in the world! Naturally each in his own way, of course. As Taro was the independent one who could tell us what he wanted without even talking, Jiro was the self-sufficient one. He could climb out of his crib by holding onto the knob of his chest of drawers with his toes and in the meantime warning himself, "Jilo, watch it!" One night he arrived in our bedroom in the dark to announce, with great clarity, "I am bloody". His father of course answered with "You must be wet." The little voice said again clearly, "bloody, not wet". And he was. He had a nose bleed. When he was two and a half he went to nursery school. He was really there on trial because there were no other young children in the neighborhood to play with. It was amazing to see how socially aware he was even at this early age. He would be playing intensely with whatever he was engaged in. Then suddenly he would look around to find one of his friends sitting alone. He would be there at once, asking if he could help him or play with him.

He is twenty-three today, but he has never lost touch for others who need him. I guess we are very lucky parents to have been blessed with two of these unusual jewels.

Finally the day arrived when we were to visit Japan. It was one of my sister-in-law's wedding. Taro was 4, Jiro two and a half. We decided to go to Los Angeles first to break up the long trip to Tokyo and to see Disney Land. This was perhaps more for the benefit of the parents, but of course the children enjoyed it very much too, except for poor Jiro when we went into the Haunted House. Something must have frightened him very much because after we come out he was stammering. We were very upset ourselves. We continued to speak slowly to him and never mentioned his stammering. He lost it within four or five months.

This showed us how easily parents can ruin their children's health. But thank God at least we could figure out what had happened and together we corrected it.

The trip was long and exhausting. Poor Jiro screamed and did not want to see anyone - not even his grandmother. As soon as we got to the hotel, we gave him a quarter of a dramamine pill and he fell asleep.

From the next morning on, he was just a regular dear little fellow. We had a great time in Japan, even thought only one person in the family spoke English. However we could understand each other with our hearts. Our children were the only Adachis to carry the

167

name, so Grandma was proud having them there. The two weeks went by very quickly. It seemed we'd only been there a few days. It was very difficult. Both boys wanted to stay in Tokyo.

On the way back we stopped in Honolulu and enjoyed a few days. At the airport the children first ran away. All the security men had to run after them. They both flopped down on the ground, determined not to leave Honolulu. We went on home with more great memories.

From then on we had lots of trips together. We went to Portugal, then again to Japan to another wedding. This time we had an even better time with our dear family and stayed almost five weeks.

The next trip took us to Yugoslavia, to Dubrovnik, where we spent three weeks and made great friends thanks to the children. These friendships have lasted throughout the years.

From there we went to Switzerland to visit the family. We were up in the Alps where my family had a chalet in Braunwald. It was a wonderful vacation for the children.

From Braunwald we finally went to Budapest where my three men really wanted to go. Masa had an international meeting, which gave us this opportunity.

It was all right for the rest of the

family, but it turned into a nightmare for me.
First the hotel could not find our room
reservations which had gone through American
Express. So we were separated into two different
wings of the hotel, Masa with Jiro and I with
Taro. We did fall asleep immediately and I'm
sure I was dreaming. I suddenly awoke with a
terrible smell of gas in my nose. I was sure
somebody was trying to kill us all. I looked at
Taro but he was sleeping peacefully. I picked
up the phone and called my husband and told him
there was the smell of gas in our room. He
picked up the sleeping Jiro and ran to our room,
only to find there was nothing. It took him
quite a while to calm me down.

Of course it was just a dream, but as I
looked out at the Danube, from our window,
everything came back to me in life size - our
jumps into that icy water to save people and all
the other horrors.

So it went all the nine days of our visit.
The city was beautiful but many buildings were
still in shambles from the 1944 bombings. Our
own apartment house and that of my grandmother's
were destroyed. It seemed that the people were
depressed and had to work very hard to keep
their jobs. The food and music were still
wonderful but that was all for me. My three men
enjoyed themselves quite well, so much so, that
when Taro was working in Vienna two years ago,
he visited Budapest with a friend and once again
enjoyed every moment of it. I just could not

169

Nina Lagergren, Raoul's sister in our "Wallenberg"
school in Brooklyn.

Lecture in high school.

With Rabbi Schudrich and husband Dr. Adachi, Tokyo Jewis Center.

New monument in Melbourne, Australia.

Street in Budapest.

New monument in Budapest.

New monument in Budapest.

cope with the air or with the new generation that made up Budapest in 1975.

As my children grew, so did Masa and I in all ways. Masa had made great strides in research. He had already received three awards and become Director of all the laboratories in his hospital. He had become well known and well respected by all.

For myself? I went back to work and worked as a school aide and my last job was as a librarian in a school.

I finally got so involved in the renewed search for Raoul Wallenberg that I have become sort of an official speaker for him, since I worked with him all those years ago in Budapest. It is always very emotional and while I speak of him, the scenes once again flash before my eyes and I end up shaken.

All over the world Wallenberg Committees are springing up and his name has become almost a household word. We try our best to let everyone know about him. We have docufilms on tape and last year there was a very successful mini-series "A Hero's Story," the story of Raoul very well done by Paramount and NBC. I was one of the advisors for the film and had the pleasure of spending three hours with Richard Chamberlain, the great actor who portrayed Raoul.

We also have a new play, written by

playwright Herb Shapiro. We have parks, walks, lanes, streets, and monuments for Raoul, but what we want is the Man himself as we believe that he is alive and we will find him. Oh what a celebration that will be!

I think I have told all - just as my dear family wanted me to - and deep in my heart I did want to tell it all. I hope that this time everybody is listening and understands, not like it was in 1945. I will keep on trying always to give my very best. I want to keep the world as beautiful as it is up here in Marlboro, surrounded by music, passion and love.

EPILOGUE

My story is finished...but not Raoul's! Soon it will be 44 years that he has been in captivity in Russia. A life time! I thought of him often and now I am in a position to finally work for him again...not as a messenger or secretary...but as a rescuer with a mission just like his. But this time it is to save one man, Raoul Wallenberg. He saved 100,000 people. Can we not save one? More importantly we must teach the young, to make them aware that one man can do so much. How much then can be done together?

I am here to try to save the children for the new world Raoul wanted so much...children who will be passionate people, caring individuals, who will look at each other as individuals, and ask only if the person is good and trustworthy or not.

Together we will hold hands all around the world for peace and friendship. When I go into schools from elementary to college, I reach many thousands of young people, who are just now finding out that out there is a real hero, a man who single-handedly saved so many. They understand what "ONE MAN" can do and are helping me to bring him back home.

We have two Raoul Wallenberg Schools, one elementary school in Brooklyn and a vocational high school in San Francisco. All these

children are living the spirit of Raoul, each
with the mind of what they can do for mankind.
We are all proud of them.

And I? I continue to speak, to spread the
word in the hope that finally someone will
listen and give our Raoul his freedom back.

There is a sequel to the epilogue...and I wish it for Raoul and not for me.

Miracles still happen. Shortly before Christmas, my younger son lost all the Christmas mail with which I had entrusted him. Imagine his great distress. Somehow I believed in a miracle and it happened. Not a "simple" miracle but one that lets you fly high!!!

A dear nun, from the order of the "Sisters of Mary Reparatrix", Women of Daring, Women of Courage, Women of Compassion, Women of Hope, Sister Kathleen Grimes, found the letters, mailed them for us and wrote me a note to tell me what had happened. Sister found the letters laying untouched on the subway seat where my Jiro had fallen asleep. She found them three or four stops from where Jiro, after waking suddenly, had jumped off the train. What an act of providence that a nun had found them!

A short while ago we visited her convent and found a new and wonderful family. Our new family prayed for my son during his 2,500 mile bicycle trip alone through the United States. With the help of their prayers he has returned unharmed and with several miracles to recount of his trip.

The sisters are always there when you need them. They always smile and give a helping hand. We are blessed.

B I O G R A P H Y

Agnes Adachi

One of Mr. Wallenberg's associates in his rescue mission in Budapest, Hungary, in 1944.

In 1945-46 she worked in Sweden in camps of survivors as a lecturer on Mr. Wallenberg's work and Swedish literary subjects.

Chairperson of Greater New York Wallenberg Committee, Inc."

Advisor to the Mini Series: "Wallenberg, A Hero's Story."

Married to a scientist, Dr. M. Adachi, has 2 sons, now living in New York.

Photo
Dr. Herb
Fischler